To R..

On t..

Ba..   012.

Love Jean and Peter.

1 Timothy 4:12

New Living Translation (NLT)

Don't let anyone think less of you
because you are young. Be an
example to all believers in what you
say, in the way you live, in your
love, your faith, and your purity.

Quiet
Reflections *for*
MORNING
and EVENING

Quiet
Reflections *for*
MORNING
and EVENING

A Devotional

Revell
a division of Baker Publishing Group
Grand Rapids, Michigan

© 2012 by Baker Publishing Group

Published by Revell
a division of Baker Publishing Group
P.O. Box 6287, Grand Rapids, MI 49516-6287
www.revellbooks.com

Originally published in 2009 as *Quiet Reflections of Hope* and *Quiet Reflections of Peace*

Combined edition published 2012

ISBN 978-0-8007-2106-0

Printed in the United States of America

Scripture is taken from GOD'S WORD ®. © 1995 God's Word to the Nations. Used by permission of Baker Publishing Group.

Produced with the assistance of The Livingstone Corporation (www.Living stoneCorp.com). Project staff includes Linda Taylor, Betsy Schmitt, Linda Washington, and Dana Niesluchowski.

12 13 14 15 16 17 18   7 6 5 4 3 2 1

In keeping with biblical principles of creation stewardship, Baker Publishing Group advocates the responsible use of our natural resources. As a member of the Green Press Initiative, our company uses recycled paper when possible. The text paper of this book is composed in part of post-consumer waste.

green
press
INITIATIVE

Welcome

God wants to welcome you into the warmth of His presence every morning—to begin your day sitting at His feet with contentment and expectation. He wants to share your joys and your sorrows and give you strength to face the day ahead. And after the day is done, the perfect way to end a day is to spend time with God—to tell Him how you spent your day and to relax in His presence as day turns to dusk. God offers encouragement and strength through His Word as you surrender your fears or frustrations.

This devotional includes 120 meditations to facilitate your time with God each morning and 120 corresponding meditations for the evening. Each meditation includes a Scripture passage and an inspirational thought to help you reflect on the truths discussed.

So every morning come and be like Mary, making what Jesus called "the right choice" (Luke 10:42). Refuse to be distracted by what lies ahead today and instead sit at Jesus' feet and focus on what you really need—a word from Him. He wants to give you quiet reflections of hope to start your day.

And as your day draws to a close, you're invited to follow in the footsteps of Nicodemus, who came to Jesus at night with his questions (John 3:2) and received insights he had never even considered! As you prepare to sink into sleep, take a few moments with your Savior. He wants to give you quiet reflections of peace to end your day.

You're welcome to stay as long as you like.

—The Editors

A New Day Dawns

God named the light day, and the darkness he named night.
There was evening, then morning—the first day.

Genesis 1:5

Day and night, night and day—a perpetual cycle instituted on the very first day of creation. Don't you love that God works in cycles? It shows in the changing of seasons, the ebb and flow of tides, and the waxing and waning of the moon. Isn't it comforting to know that bleak winter melts into glorious spring, that the valley floor ascends to the mountaintop, and that darkness is chased away by the light?

Even the very darkest day of all, the Friday of Jesus' death, was resolved in a sublime early morning a few days later. Through pain, persecution, and crucifixion, Jesus knew the outcome all along. That hope, that promise from His Father God, saw Him through His dark night and tinged His proclamation on the cross, "It is finished!" with a resounding note of triumph.

That hope is now your hope. His crown of thorns was traded for a crown of glory . . . so yours will be. His wounded, beaten, and crushed body was restored . . . so yours will be.

His sorrow marked a dark period, but oh, did joy ever come with the morning! And so it will be for you as you cling to that amazing promise that dark is always followed by light for God's children, a hint He wrote across the sky on that very first day. Welcome and bask in the divine light He provides you on this brand new morning.

As Numerous as Stars

He took Abram outside and said, "Now look up at the sky and count the stars, if you are able to count them." He also said to him, "That's how many descendants you will have!"

Genesis 15:5

Stretched out on a blanket in the cool crisp grass late in the summer evening, you gaze into the night sky. In the country, away from the glare of city or suburbia, the stars stand out, vivid and bright. As stars blend into galaxies upon galaxies, it is impossible to count them.

Imagine Abram staring into that same night sky thousands of years ago. He, too, had a wish. For a child, a descendant to carry on the family name and tradition. Yet, when God promised him that he and Sarai would have as many descendants as the stars in the night sky, well, that was too much to hope for. They were too old. Their time was running out. Impossible, they thought.

Has God spoken something into the still of your soul and you are just wishing it will come to pass? Or like Abram and Sarai, you think time has run out for you. You can't imagine how such a thing will ever come true for you. You are left wishing for a shooting star.

Tonight, put your faith in God alone and rest. The writer of Hebrews reminds you, "Faith assures us of things we expect and convinces us of the existence of things we cannot see" (Hebrews 11:1).

As you gaze into the beauty and mystery of the night sky, raise your hopes and dreams to God. Wait on Him to bestow blessings on you as numerous as the stars in the sky.

7

Letters to God

Hezekiah took the letters from the messengers, read them, and went to the LORD's temple. He spread them out in front of the LORD and prayed to the LORD. "LORD of Armies, God of Israel, you are enthroned over the angels. . . . Turn your ear toward me, LORD, and listen."

2 Kings 19:14–16

Do you feel, as Hezekiah did so many years ago, that this is "a day filled with misery, punishment, and disgrace" (2 Kings 19:3)? Life sometimes crashes in, leaving nothing but hopelessness in its wake. Is a broken relationship, poor health, or an unbearable situation crushing your spirit? If so, this morning's Scripture is for you.

Sennacherib, king of Assyria, struck fear in the hearts of the Israelites. His army had captured every city except Jerusalem. Confident that he would also conquer Judah, Sennacherib taunted the Israelites. He hoped to instill in the Israelites a fear of the enemy that was stronger than their faith in God.

Hezekiah took the life-threatening letters of ultimatum delivered by Sennacherib's messengers and spread them out before the Lord in His temple. And he prayed, asking God to turn His ear toward him and listen to his request. Hezekiah knew that without God's intervention, the city of Jerusalem could not hold its own against the mighty Assyrian army. But Hezekiah knew that God's power could trump that of any invading army. Instead of being terrified, King Hezekiah held fast to what he knew to be true about his God.

When troubles arise and your faith begins to falter, your God stands ready to help. Spread out your request before God and pray that He will listen. Remember that His power is mightier than any battle you face today.

One Smooth Stone

The LORD is my rock and my fortress and my Savior, my God, my rock in whom I take refuge, my shield, the strength of my salvation, my stronghold, my refuge, and my Savior who saved me from violence. The LORD should be praised.

2 Samuel 22:2–4

Five smooth stones were used. But only one was needed.

For forty days, Goliath, a nine-foot-tall Philistine giant, mocked the Israelites and their God. Brave warriors were terrified of what Goliath could do.

Young David arrived on the scene and was instantly outraged by Goliath's remarks. While his brother tried to discourage him from getting involved, David was stirred by his confidence in God. With five smooth stones and his sling in hand, David set out to conquer his enemy in the name of the Lord God Almighty. Knowing that the Lord would deliver him from his enemy, David triumphed with just one small stone.

Years later, after facing many enemies, David used the rock image in a psalm describing his confidence in God. God was his rock—the only one needed to defeat any enemy (Psalm 18). God delivered David from all of his enemies and made him king over Israel. Therefore, David could rest the full weight of his trust in God.

What enemies are taunting you tonight? Maybe your giant is your health, finances, addictions, a hectic schedule, or rebellious children. Such enemies taunt us and rob us of sleep. When trouble beckons, call on the Lord God Almighty. As your rock, fortress, and shield, He is a source of strength. Run to Him for shelter.

The battle is the Lord's. With faith in God, you will triumph.

God's Refrigerator Art

*Moses called Bezalel and Oholiab and every other craftsman
to whom the LORD had given these skills and who was willing
to come and do the work.*

Exodus 36:2

Your preschool daughter clutches a fat purple crayon in her hand.
Her arm is sweeping across the paper as she fills a fresh sheet
of white paper with colorful circles. Her joyous effort looks like
fireworks on a warm summer night. She offers it to you proudly.

"For me? Thank you!" you respond, giving her a hug. "I
have the perfect spot for this." You head to the refrigerator and
use a couple of magnets to position her offering so everyone in your
home can admire it.

In ancient Israel, two men named Bezalel and Oholiab spent
their childhood years faithfully growing in their skills as artisans.
By the time they were adults, God called upon them to lead the crew
of master craftsmen who would create the interior of the worship
center for the nation. However, Bezalel and Oholiab's skills were
not the sole reason for their divine job assignment; these men had
also distinguished themselves because they'd been faithful to the
Lord. (Bezalel, in fact, is the first person named in Scripture said
to be filled with the Spirit of God.) Their work was an offering of
love, flowing out of their relationship with God.

He welcomes the gifts your unique skills create the same way
you celebrate the crayoned artwork of your child. He celebrates
your offering and places it in the perfect spot to reflect His glory.
Whatever tasks you face today, ask God to show you how you can
use your gifts and glorify Him in the process.

Fearless

God didn't give us a cowardly spirit but a spirit of power, love, and good judgment.

2 Timothy 1:7

Fear. According to psychologists, it is one of the most powerful emotions we can experience. It can cause us to take drastic action or paralyze us into inaction. It can make us lose sleep, lose weight, and lose reason. In short; it can control us.

Life seems to be filled with perils—real or only anticipated. A conflict with your husband. A scheduled meeting with your child's principal. An overdue bill in the mail. We often fear what we don't know or even what we think might happen.

Are you plagued by fear tonight about what will happen tomorrow? As you lay in the cold grip of fear, remember that spirit of fear didn't come from God. So where did it come from? We have a powerful enemy who whispers into our thoughts and fuels emotions of dread, worry, helplessness, and fear.

Take back control! As the apostle Paul explained to his spiritual son, Timothy, God has given you a spirit of "power, love and good judgment." That means you can handle any situation with His help. Be confident in His promise and cover yourself in a blanket of God's love as soon as your head touches the pillow tonight. Rest in God's ability to conquer the spirit of fear.

Following the Rainbow

I will put my rainbow in the clouds to be a sign of my promise to the earth.

Genesis 9:13

Do you remember the first time your eyes caught sight of a rainbow arching through the afternoon sky? The rain beat down on the pavement followed by the stripes of God's love gleaming through the newly sunlit atmosphere after the drifting clouds shifted—truly a wondrous sight! Your childhood imagination was surely set on finding the treasure at the end of the multicolored trail.

Following the path to the rainbow's end with your eyes may have been fun as a child, but as a beautiful woman of God, the multihued exhibit signifies so much more than an appealing display. God created this dramatic miracle as a sign and a promise to all the earth that we will never again be destroyed in a flood such as in Noah's day.

Noah was not a fairy-tale character; he was a follower of God Most High who obediently built the ark just as the Lord had instructed. Noah and his small family became faith-filled pioneers of a new beginning for the earth—and for you and me. That rainbow you have chased more than once in your life is a promise to you of God's mercy and love.

His love is unfailing and unceasing. Today, as you start your day, praise God for His abundant love for you and His mercy toward the earth.

Looking Back for Hope

Lovingly, you will lead the people you have saved. Powerfully, you will guide them to your holy dwelling.

Exodus 15:13

After leaving a life of slavery in Egypt, the people of Israel traveled to the Red Sea, only to be trapped by the sea with the Egyptian army in pursuit. Their situation had now moved from hopeful to hopeless.

Or so it seemed.

In the midst of their helplessness, God provided a path through the Red Sea. He then caused the Egyptian army to drown in the sea—thus saving the people of Israel (see Exodus 14).

Moses and the people celebrated the victory by singing the song from which today's verse is derived. They knew God would continue to provide for His people, just as He always provided. He would lead them to the Promised Land. They had only to remember their past to find comfort in their present.

Think back to the times that you have seen God move powerfully in your life. How did He work in ways that seemed impossible at the time? Sadly, we sometimes take for granted the things He has done. Or, we think we have to fight the battles on our own and forget that our loving Father can and will provide for His children.

Tonight, in the midst of life and all its uncertainties, consider God's promise of guidance. He will never start you on a journey only to abandon you in the middle of it. Tonight, let the words of assurance spoken by Moses guide you to a place of rest.

Salty

They were appointed to stand to give thanks and praise to the
LORD every morning. They were appointed to do the same
thing in the evening.

1 Chronicles 23:30

Daily the Levites performed many tasks in the temple of God.
Ordinary jobs included baking the special bread used in the temple.
Special rituals included preparing for the reverential sacrifices
on holy days. Two of their daily appointed jobs, thanksgiving
and praise, salted everything, flavoring every mundane task and
every traditionally rich service. In thanking and praising God every
morning and every evening, even the dullest of their routine tasks
became worship.

What a recipe of rich spiritual growth for each of us! Sup-
pose you made a daily appointment to praise and thank God each
morning, asking that every task of the day become "salted" with
worship? The senior citizen in front of you at the supermarket
would become an opportunity to serve and not a temptation to
become impatient. A whining child might give cause for thanks
that she could cry and you could hear. The fantastic miracle of
Christ's love that you realize on Sunday would not so easily flee
from your heart, crushed by the beatings of Monday's mundane.
Each morning appointment with God might cause you to be more
cognizant of God's moving because you would know that daily it
is your responsibility to find something for which to be grateful.

So rise, meet that daily appointment of praising and thanking
the Lord. Enjoy your newly flavored walk with Him more fully!

Sweet Sleep

When you lie down, you will not be afraid. As you lie there, your sleep will be sweet.

Proverbs 3:24

You know the days when you wake up refreshed after a good night's rest. You feel as if you can conquer the world! But there are some nights where you feel overwhelmed by what tomorrow may bring. With the day's worries running through your mind, it is impossible to close your eyes and rest. Sweet sleep eludes you.

The anxiety that comes as a result of a busy, chaotic world is nothing new. As you read through the Bible, you learn about many people who were also burdened by anxieties, distractions, and fear. Perhaps that's why wise King Solomon included the above promise in his wisdom advice. He knew that peace was one of the promises God gave to Israel during their time in the wilderness (see Leviticus 26:6). If your heart is at war, peaceful sleep is difficult to gain.

That's why Solomon highlighted the value of clinging to the wisdom of God. As we trust God, our "sleep will be sweet."

God knows you need sound slumber to feel refreshed. Meditate on the verse above. Remember that God provides you with a quiet place of rest for a sweet sleep that refreshes.

A Touch of Encouragement

The Almighty LORD *will teach me what to say, so I will know how to encourage weary people. Morning after morning he will wake me to listen like a student.*

Isaiah 50:4

This verse says that God awakens you "morning after morning," wanting to teach you as a teacher with a student. The context of this passage is the Lord's special servant describing His obedience in contrast to the disobedience of God's people, Israel. Because this servant is willing to learn, God promises to teach. This servant will bring special encouragement to God's weary people.

The passage works for believers as well. God willingly wakes you morning after morning, wanting to teach you. He has a message for a world in sorrow and pain, and the message comes through the hands, feet, and mouths of His followers. The Lord desires that you be His light in the dark world, bringing the kind of encouragement only God can give to people weary of sin and suffering.

So many people need encouragement. Often it can be difficult to even be aware when someone has a need or, if you are aware, to know what to say or how to help. So it makes sense to pay attention in God's classroom this morning. Ask God to show you, as you walk through your day today, who could use a kind word, a soft touch, a big hug, even a simple smile and a thank you. A little encouragement can bring sunshine into someone's dark world.

What can you do to bring encouragement into your world today?

A Tough Climb

Listen to my cry for help, O God. Pay attention to my prayer.
From the ends of the earth, I call to you when I begin to lose
heart. Lead me to the Rock that is high above me.

Psalm 61:1–2

Sometimes at night, small problems can loom like giant mountains. Even goals we set, which were not meant to be problems, can seem overwhelming. The challenge then turns into a frustration that causes you to lose heart.

Consider the discipline it takes to climb a mountain. Even if you've never climbed one, you can appreciate the struggle up that rocky face and the triumph of reaching the top. Many times during the journey, a climber might be tempted to give up.

Reaching a goal can seem like climbing a mountain. David, the shepherd turned king, was no stranger to the challenges of life. After all, he spent over a decade on the run from King Saul who wanted him dead. After being anointed king and finally ascending the throne, David's goal was to unite all of Israel. But David knew that the challenge of ruling a divided people could be surmounted by God, "the Rock that is high above." God was his place of refuge and strength.

If your commitment is waning, cry out to God just as David did. From the ends of the earth He will hear your prayer. He knows that your goal is a tough climb and offers His help. Each step you take together brings you one step closer to conquering your goal.

When you're frustrated and feeling overwhelmed by the challenges along the way, turn to God, your Rock, to help you. From the ends of the earth, He will answer.

17

God's System

Have you ever given orders to the morning or assigned a place for the dawn?

Job 38:12

Every book has an assigned place at the library. Each novel, biography, or science fiction has its own call number that tells the librarian where the book should be placed. Each shelf holds specific books in a specific order. Without organization, a library would be total chaos—piles of books strewn across shelves. Without a system, books would become almost unusable for no one could find what they needed. Organization makes all that information easy to find and available.

Imagine the universe without organization—the earth orbiting at whatever speed in whatever orbit, leaving some of us to freeze and others to scorch. Or what if the seasons came and went in whatever order they wanted, whenever they wanted? What if you never knew whether spring, summer, or fall would follow winter—or if winter would end at all? Fortunately, God has a system of organization. He has precisely designated the location of each star and calculated the rotation of each planet. In the midst of this system, He has "assigned a place for the dawn."

If God can keep the universe in order, surely He can help you handle your day. Like an extremely well-organized library, nothing goes amiss with Him in charge. Sip your coffee, watch the sun rise, and let Him take care of the order of your life.

Sleep Tight, Little One

He will not let you fall. Your guardian will not fall asleep.
Indeed, the Guardian of Israel never rests or sleeps.

Psalm 121:3–4

If you have children, you've probably spent many nights watching over them as they slept—especially when they were babies. Perhaps you have little ones right now. You watch their every exhale and inhale and make sure they are comfortable. You can't take your eyes off their small frames as they lie there nestled in bed. Perhaps you pray they will have sweet dreams and feel secure as they sleep. Quietly you whisper, "Sleep tight, little one. Sleep tight."

Don't you long for someone to have that kind of watchful care over you? The security that you provide your little ones is only a fraction of what your heavenly Father provides for you. As the psalmist explains, the Lord is "your guardian." Because He never sleeps, He can offer protection throughout the night. He will never take His eyes off of you.

Restful sleep comes with knowing that you're cared for. Problems during the day have a tendency to crowd our minds. We find ourselves counting sheep and worries. That's why it's great to know that a big God watches over you. He can handle those worries while you sleep. His watchful love says to you, "Sleep tight."

Lay your head down, close your eyes, and know that the Maker of the Universe, Creator of the Heavens, and the Guardian of Israel is up tonight watching over you. "The eyes of the Lord are everywhere" (Proverbs 15:3).

His Quiet Glory

*In the morning, O LORD, hear my voice. In the morning I lay
my needs in front of you, and I wait.*

Psalm 5:3

Whether hiking, biking, or just sleeping out, surely a great pleasure of life is to curl up in a sleeping bag under the stars. If you
awake in the early morning before the sun has risen, before your
companions are stirring, before coffee and bacon and eggs, there
is a hush over the world. Droplets of dew rest on your sleeping bag
and it seems like the night is still very much around you.

Then slowly, silently, almost imperceptibly, you begin to see
a change in the sky. You can't put your finger on it, but the stars
seem to fade and the inky blackness lightens into a cold gray. Then
gradually the gray takes on warmer hues. None of this happens
quickly. Everything seems to be holding its breath for something.
Suddenly, brilliantly, a bright light highlights the edges of the
hills. The sun has risen, with all of its beauty, promise, and hope.

Whether it is still dark outside or you're reading these words
with the sun already moving up the sky, take these moments to
come before God, offering Him your entire day. As you bring Him
praise and lay your needs before Him, take just a few moments to
wait. Listen. Breathe. In those moments, God's Spirit will imperceptibly relax your heart and feed your soul. You may not be able
to pinpoint the moment it happens, but you'll know, when you
arise to take on the day, that God has touched you with His light.

Finding Rest

When I lie down, I ask, "When will I get up?" But the evening is long, and I'm exhausted from tossing about until dawn.

Job 7:4

Job had every reason to complain. His children had died, his wealth was gone, and his body was covered with painful boils (Job 1–2). He was miserable during the day, and the nights seemed unbearably long as he tossed and turned, unable to find relief.

Job was ready to give up. Although he was a righteous man with faith in God, sleeplessness brought him to a breaking point; he had lost hope. But God—his Hope—never lost track of Job. Even though He allowed the pain in Job's life, God still loved Job and later gave him rest from all of his pain and anxieties.

Sleepless nights—whether from illness, children, anxiety, or any other source—can cause us to lose perspective and to forget our Hope. We find ourselves feeling hopeless in the wee hours.

Feeling a loss of hope? The Father cares about you and has promised, again and again, to give you rest. In Matthew 11:28, he calls, "Come to me, all who are tired from carrying heavy loads, and I will give you rest."

Tonight may be long and possibly sleepless. But don't give up hope. If you toss and turn, instead of being frustrated, use that time to recall songs of praise or to repeat a verse that comforts you. Remember that your Father loves you more than you could ever imagine. He has promised to comfort you through hard times and will give you rest.

Unexpected Showers

*We wait for the LORD. He is our help and our shield. In him
our hearts find joy. In his holy name we trust. Let your mercy
rest on us, O LORD, since we wait with hope for you.*

Psalm 33:20–22

Look down on any city street on a rainy day and you'll see a
colorful sea of umbrellas—portable roofs keeping the elements
at bay. Yellow, pink, clear, striped, even Impressionist-painting-
themed umbrellas jostle against basic black as people make their
way through the rain to their next destination. A few people, here
and there, got caught without an umbrella and so use a purse or
newspaper as they scamper as fast as they can to avoid the raindrops. Most everyone (except for the occasional free spirit) looks
to shield hair and clothing from the rain.

When trials and difficulties pour down all around you and it
seems like troubles rain from the dark sky, God says that He is
your help and shield. Like an umbrella, He covers and protects
you from the worst of the storm. Whatever drips into your life
today, your Lord is there to help keep you warm, safe, and dry.
You don't have to worry or fret because He is protecting you.

As you venture out today—whether the sky is sunny or
whether dark clouds threaten—don't forget your "umbrella." In
that, your heart can find joy. In Him, you can trust. His mercy
will rest on you because you wait with hope for Him.

Be Gone, Gloom

He uncovers mysteries hidden in the darkness and brings gloom into the light.

Job 12:22

If you've ever been camping, you know the comfort of a roaring campfire. Not only is it great for roasting marshmallows and making s'mores, it also chases away the gloom of darkness. Sitting by the glowing flames, you can't help feeling safer. Noises of animals off into the distance don't sound as threatening.

In a dark place, every shadow or noise can seem threatening. That's why kids often imagine monsters coming out of closets and crave a night-light. But such fears aren't just the province of children. The "monsters" in our closets aren't the cuddly ones from *Monsters Inc.* but real anxieties we carry to bed. Like children, we crave a light that will drive away the darkness.

Times of great testing are the dark times when we most need the light of understanding. Job faced such a time after losing all of his children, his crops, and his health. Although the time was dark and he didn't understand the reasons behind his suffering, Job knew a source of light. As he explained to his judgmental friend, Zophar, God is the light that reveals mysteries and parts the darkness. No secret is hidden from Him.

Perhaps you're in a time of darkness that you don't fully understand. To release gloom and fear, turn to the Light. Best of all, this Light never needs to be plugged in!

Your Backpack

Thanks be to the Lord, who daily carries our burdens for us. God is our salvation.

Psalm 68:19

The elementary school starts at nine o'clock in the morning. Groups of children make their way along the neighborhood sidewalks. Occasionally a mom walks alongside a very young child, providing safety and security from the doorway at home to the school entrance. Sometimes the child's backpack just gets too heavy for the walk and he passes it off to his mom—whose shoulders are much bigger and stronger. As they walk to school together, mom carries the burden and the little boy skips along beside her.

A child's backpack holds the necessities of the day—schoolbooks, pencils, paper, bag lunch—but even so, sometimes it's just too heavy for his little shoulders. What are you carrying with you today? What's in your "backpack"? Worries about money, discontent in a difficult relationship, or maybe concern for an elderly relative? Perhaps you carry sadness, grief, or anger. Sometimes strong emotions can become extremely heavy, but any burden—whether great or small—can impede your freedom to be the person God wants you to be.

When your burden gets too heavy, remember that your heavenly Father walks on the sidewalk of life beside you, always willing and anxious to carry your heavy load. So get rid of that backpack! Hand it over! And once you pass your burden on to Him, you will be free to skip along beside Him, and maybe even do a few cartwheels!

Blanketed in His Care

I fall asleep in peace the moment I lie down because you alone,
O LORD, enable me to live securely.

Psalm 4:8

We all know people who can fall asleep anytime, anyplace—from the dentist's chair to the back end of a roaring Harley. But most of us have to ease into slumber, letting the momentum of the day wind down and tumble off our shoulders. Can you relate?

Sometimes that restful state eludes us, not just for a few minutes as we settle in, but deep into the night. When we do fall asleep, it is fitful and strained, not bringing refreshment on the following day.

Whether we are preoccupied with our dwindling bank account, worried about the results of a blood test, or disturbed by a comment uttered by the boss, resting is not in the night's equation. But there is an antidote—a remedy for unrest. It comes in the form of a cozy blanket that covers us with safety and warms us with peace. Where do we get it? There is one exclusive source: "You alone, O LORD, enable me to live securely." Only God is able to drape us with peace and assurance in the midst of thoughts or circumstances that lead to sleepless nights. Ask Him and believe what the psalmist knew as you drift off to peaceful sleep.

Your Perfect Help

*I look up toward the mountains. Where can I find help? My
help comes from the LORD, the maker of heaven and earth. . . .
The LORD guards you as you come and go, now and forever.*

Psalm 121:1–2, 8

"My help comes from the LORD, the maker of heaven and earth."
Did you catch that? The Father God, the Alpha and Omega, the
Great I AM is the source of your help. No better source of help
exists anywhere.

Think of times in your life when there was no help anywhere
you turned. Remember the times when you sought help from
sources that just didn't provide any help at all. People disappointed
you. The solutions you tried came up empty. You felt alone. At
times it seemed even that God had retreated from you.

The psalmist says to fix your gaze on the majestic horizon.
What you've been aching for all along lies there. Matthew 6:33
issues the perfect reminder: "First, be concerned about his kingdom and what has his approval." With your focus and trust directed heavenward, everything—yes, every single thing—will
fall into place.

Do you need help with a wayward child or spouse? The Creator
has a plan. Do you feel powerless in a situation at work or in the
community? Your Abba Father knows it and He's got your back.
Financial issues? God promises to meet your needs. As today's
verse indicates, He will watch over your comings and goings
and will be there to protect you. Lift your eyes to the high places
today; your help is now cresting the summit.

Turning Point

I am worn out from my groaning. My eyes flood my bed every night. I soak my couch with tears. My eyes blur from grief. . . . The LORD has heard the sound of my crying. The LORD has heard my plea for mercy. The LORD accepts my prayer.

Psalm 6:6–9

When we're feeling ill and are alone, the night can loom long and seem especially miserable.

David, the psalmist, wrote about such a night, one in which he was tired, alone, and miserable due to an illness and the taunts of his enemies. With no relief in sight, he could only weep.

Many of us stop right there—at the sound of our depressed weeping. But David didn't stop. Instead, as he wrestled with his pain, he reached a turning point. Toward the end of his psalm, he wrote, "The LORD has heard my plea for mercy. The LORD accepts my prayer" (Psalm 6:9). Remembering the Lord's presence and power, he found hope and rest.

Is there something troubling you tonight? Perhaps you're facing an issue that causes the tears to spring to your eyes. Or perhaps this is one of a long series of sleepless nights where you wonder if the morning will ever come. Know that your Father is there with you. He hears you, loves you, and will answer. May you, like David, see your life reach a turning point.

Treasure God's Word

I wholeheartedly searched for you. Do not let me wander away from your commandments. I have treasured your promise in my heart so that I may not sin against you.

Psalm 119:10–11

What do you treasure most? Is it a special piece of jewelry? A photograph album? A chest filled with mementos of days gone by?

Jesus spoke of treasures once when He said, "Store up treasures for yourselves in heaven, where moths and rust don't destroy and thieves don't break in and steal. Your heart will be where your treasure is" (Matthew 6:20–21). The psalmist said that he had treasured God's promise in his heart so that he would not sin.

The best way to treasure God's Word in your heart is to learn it and memorize it so that it's ready at hand when you need it. By taking a verse or two and patiently working it into your mind and heart, your responses and attitudes begin to change. They will line up with God's way of doing things.

Take an index card and write down a verse that is relevant to your life today. Put the card in your purse and carry it with you this week as you work to memorize the verse. After a short time, you'll find that God's Word will begin to saturate your mind and influence your behavior.

When you take the time and effort to memorize the Bible, it means that you treasure God's Word. And that treasure is for keeps.

A Little Night Music

The LORD commands his mercy during the day, and at night his song is with me—a prayer to the God of my life.

Psalm 42:8

In the middle of the night, what sounds do you hear? Crickets chirping, cars rushing by, train whistles, wind rustling in the trees, a baby's soft breathing over the monitor? They are the music of the night—music that lulls us to sleep. These sounds are soothing, because we expect to hear them.

Some people enjoy the quiet sound of wind chimes making their random tunes as played by the soft night breezes. There's something about their soft, cheerful tune that makes the night seem less gloomy. Nighttime music, to be effective, has to be soothing and predictable. Otherwise, you can't get to sleep. So you don't expect blaring horns, squealing guitars, discordant notes, or anything unexpected.

One of the sons of Korah—one of the musicians King David put in charge of worship at the tabernacle—penned a soothing psalm—Psalm 42. Its lyrics are a litany of praise for times of discouragement. For example: "Why are you discouraged, my soul? Why are you so restless? Put your hope in God, because I will still praise him. He is my savior and my God" (Psalm 42:5).

Discouragement sounds a discordant note in our lives. We feel out of sorts and everything turns colorless. Praise has a way of dispelling the darkness. If you find yourself tossing and turning, consider a little night music: Psalm 42. Make it a prayer to the God of your life.

Morning Surrender

I cry out to you for help, O LORD, and in the morning my prayer will come into your presence.

Psalm 88:13

The freshness of a brand-new morning is the perfect time to communicate with God. C. S. Lewis wrote about the importance of prayer and surrender at the beginning of each day before your wishes and desires rush in and take over. Lewis compared our voices to wild animals and described the process as pushing your voice back so as to be able to hear God's other, quieter voice.

Prayer and listening take effort and intention. You learn to do them, however, only by practicing. So this morning, as you begin your day, talk to God. With the psalmist, let your prayer come into His presence this morning.

Get a fresh piece of paper or a new notebook and write to God. Thank Him for the gift of a new day and intentionally surrender it back to His care. Make a list of the things you need or want to get done. Then offer your list to God. Ask Him to guide your steps today and to show you when to allow "divine appointments" to interrupt your schedule. Allow God to design your day, and then receive His plans gladly. Try to make this part of your morning routine.

As you leave all the day's plans to God, your perspective changes. Stress melts away because you no longer need to control or manipulate what happens. Instead, you step into the day knowing that you and God are on the same page, and you're walking in His will.

God's Grandeur

*Let go of your concerns! Then you will know that I am God.
I rule the nations. I rule the earth.*

Psalm 46:10

It's so easy to get wrapped up in the busyness of our lives. The
laundry piles up. There are the dishes, endless household chores,
work problems, and all the responsibilities of being a modern
woman. The list seems to go on and on! We find ourselves trying
to hold it all together in our minds.

But we are called to let go, and be still, as this day comes to
an end. When we set aside the "to do" lists and seek quiet—then
our hearts, eyes, and minds will be free. Silence and emptiness
opens up "mind space" in order to give God some room.

All we need to do is look beyond ourselves toward the stars
above. Then we will recognize how small our lives truly are. How
puny are those concerns that seemed so big only moments ago!
They are dwarfed by the vastness of the galaxy created by God.

Consider also the openness of the vast plains and desert lands.
Areas like the Grand Canyon or the Badlands are nothing to the
vastness of the Creator—the One who rules the earth.

God has placed us in an orderly universe, on a beautiful planet,
surrounded by gently waving trees, tucked in at night by a jew-
eled sky.

Look up, and you will be able to let go. We don't have to rule
the world. That's God's job!

The Distant Shore

If I climb upward on the rays of the morning sun or land on the most distant shore of the sea where the sun sets, even there your hand would guide me and your right hand would hold on to me.

Psalm 139:9–10

What problems are you facing today? As you sip your cup of morning coffee and reflect on the tough issues you face, don't forget that the Lord's presence is inescapable; all of creation bears witness to His handiwork. God will help you navigate across the sea of your life and He'll never be too far away to rescue you from danger.

Are you stuck in the middle of what feels like a never-ending storm of strife and trouble? Heartache and pain? Illness or crisis? Do you feel like reaching out for a hand to hold, like your boat is about to tip over due to the raging waves of chaos? This verse reveals to us that the Lord is holding out His hand. The Lord is waiting for you to grab on to His strong grip and allow Him to guide you to the shore.

Psalm 139 is packed full of assurance that the Lord is present and active, no matter how wild your moments of life may seem. There's no escaping the all-powerful love of God. He's crazy about you! In your troubles, God promises to be your support, guiding you and holding you tight through life's toughest storms.

Your merciful Lord and Savior will be faithful to carry you safely to the shore, just in time to enjoy a beautiful sunset this evening. As you begin your day, have confidence in knowing that God is not only on your side but that He is guiding you and holding you tight.

A God Who Listens

*I love the LORD because he hears my voice, my pleas for mercy.
I will call on him as long as I live because he turns his ear
toward me.*

Psalm 116:1–2

The value of a listening ear is immeasurable, especially when we
have a need to share. Consider the last time you really felt heard
and understood. Even if a problem you related didn't automatically
disappear, perhaps you felt better, knowing that you were heard.

We all long for someone who not only listens, but also understands us and truly wants to hear what we're saying. Many
children seek a listening ear at the wrong time sometimes, in
our opinion! They catch us when we're on the phone or trying
to get to sleep. At those times, we might brush off their concerns
as trivial. "Can't it wait till morning?" we say. But when the
shoe is on the other foot and we're longing for a listening ear,
no concern of ours seems trivial. And some nighttime concerns
cannot wait until the morning. We need someone to listen—and
listen good—right now.

The writer of Psalm 116 has good news: there is a listening ear
that is always tuned to you. That ear belongs to God. Just as the
psalmist clung to the God who hears, we, too, can be comforted,
knowing that when we pray we aren't ignored nor do we have to
compete for attention.

Isn't it amazing? God, the Creator of heaven and earth, listens
to you: your frustrations, tiredness, or confusion. He celebrates
with you your joys, triumphs, excitement, and hope. Come to
Him now, knowing that He wants to hear your voice.

In the Starting Blocks

The eternal God, the LORD, the Creator of the ends of the earth, doesn't grow tired or become weary. His understanding is beyond reach. He gives strength to those who grow tired and increases the strength of those who are weak. . . . The strength of those who wait with hope in the LORD will be renewed. They will soar on wings like eagles. They will run and won't become weary. They will walk and won't grow tired.

Isaiah 40:28–31

At a track meet, even the spectators in the stands can sense the tension the runners experience in the moments before the starter's pistol is fired. As each racer plants her feet in the starting blocks, her physical posture of readiness is the fastest, most effective way to launch into her run. Those still, expectant seconds in the blocks give the runner an opportunity to intensely focus on the course before her, until . . .

Bang! The pistol is fired and she explodes into the race.

Though a racer's job is all about motion, those moments paused and waiting in the starting blocks are essential to running her race well. Your own busy agenda holds the temptation to simply rush into your day. These moments of prayer in your morning are your opportunity to plant your feet in the starting blocks and seek God's supernatural strength and understanding for the race of your everyday life.

Offer yourself to God today, laying all of your needs, concerns and hopes at His feet, then take a few moments to simply wait on Him in silence. By first placing yourself in a posture of waiting readiness with Him, you'll be prepared to run today's race well.

Repeat, Repeat, Repeat

Teach them to your children, and talk about them when you're at home or away, when you lie down or get up.

Deuteronomy 11:19

If you have children, what are some of the ways you help them learn? Perhaps you sounded out each word or letter over and over as you taught your child to read or patiently demonstrated each stitch as you taught the child to sew. Repetition is one of the ways we learned to read, play the piano, swim, drive a car, and so on. Repeating an action or a word ensures that you won't forget it.

As the people of Israel prepared to occupy the Promised Land, Moses, like a good parent, wanted to impart some final words of wisdom, since he would not be with them when they crossed the River Jordan. So, he reminded them to be faithful to God and teach His ways to their children. They could do this by repeating God's laws to themselves over and over—wherever they went. If they ran into problems, rehearsing God's promises would serve as a reminder of God's presence, power, and peace.

Worry is a hazard that causes us to forget the other perspectives and options we have. That's why repeating God's promises is a preventive measure, one that works to chase away the blahs.

As you prepare to lie down tonight, think about the signs and wonders God has worked in your life. Recall too the awesome history of our faith, culminating in the Word who became man in order to save us. These images can inspire us to a renewed commitment to obedience.

Shine On!

You are light for the world. . . . Let your light shine in front of people. Then they will see the good that you do and praise your Father in heaven.

Matthew 5:14–16

If you're an early riser, you probably flipped on a light in your bathroom or kitchen without thinking much about it. We are able to bring light into the darkness with such ease, aren't we?

Jesus shared the words above with an audience used to working very, very hard to generate a different kind of light in their lives. Many of His hearers longed to reflect God's goodness and purity. The only way they could dream of creating a light-filled life with God was by following long lists of do's and don'ts. It was almost as if they were lightbulbs trying to glow while being completely disconnected from their source of power.

Jesus turned those futile efforts upside down with His words, "You are light for the world." He wanted His hearers to know that doing good always flows out of a connection to Him, rather than trying to create a connection by performing lists of righteous acts.

You don't need to try to generate your own current. He is your power source. As you are connected to Him, you can't do anything except shine. His life automatically flows through you like electricity flows through a lightbulb.

Is there a lamp or fixture near you this morning? Turn the light on for a moment and enjoy the simplicity of the bulb's glow. Connected to its power source, it shines. And today, so can you!

Waiting with Hope

Wait with hope for the LORD. Be strong, and let your heart be courageous. Yes, wait with hope for the LORD.

Psalm 27:14

We live in a fast-paced, instant-gratification culture, where waiting is seen as a bad thing. We don't like waiting at red lights or for trains to pass. But the Bible describes many instances of God patiently waiting before acting. Over four hundred years passed before God freed the people of Israel from slavery in Egypt. He waited over a millennium after that before sending His Son to earth. And he's still waiting for just the right time for that Son to return to Earth to claim His people.

David, the writer of Psalm 27, majored in waiting. Many years passed between his being anointed king (1 Samuel 16:13) and his ascending to the throne (2 Samuel 5). In Psalm 27:14, he repeats the same message twice: "wait with hope for the Lord." David took his own advice during the long years of running from Saul and various enemies.

What are you waiting on tonight? A wayward child to come home? A spouse to come back to your marriage emotionally or physically? A job that will pay the bills? Waiting can be difficult. Yet we do not wait in despair. We can wait with the hope that God is restoring our lives and is working things out for our good (Romans 8:28). So before you close your eyes tonight, ask God to help you wait for Him to move in specific areas in your life. Then, fall asleep with hope in your heart, knowing that God will hear your prayer.

Your To-Do List

Everything you say or do should be done in the name of the Lord Jesus, giving thanks to God the Father through him.

Colossians 3:17

What does your "to-do" list look like for today? Are you already stressing about the time it will take you to get everything done? How are you going to do these mundane tasks "in the name of the Lord Jesus, giving thanks to God the Father"? After all, it's just a to-do list—groceries, dry cleaning, work tasks, errands. How can these possibly make a difference to Jesus?

Anything that concerns you concerns Jesus. Anything on your list today is important to Him. Yes, it may seem mundane, but if you remember who you are and why you're still walking on the planet, you'll remember that every day is a divine appointment, every task is a divine opportunity to do it in the name of Jesus.

Go to the grocery store? Maybe you'll unexpectedly meet a friend in the cereal aisle and can follow up on a prayer request from a few weeks back. Pick up dry cleaning? An opportunity to smile and thank the harried woman behind the counter. Work tasks? A chance to do your job well, help your co-workers, serve a client, meet a need. Errands? You never know what might await around the corner—even if it's an opportunity to learn patience in line at the post office!

Every step of your day can be done "in the name of the Lord Jesus." He desires that you glorify Him with every moment of your day. With Jesus, the opportunities will arise without any trouble at all.

Pour Out Your Heart

My salvation and my glory depend on God. God is the rock of my strength, my refuge. Trust him at all times, you people. Pour out your hearts in his presence. God is our refuge.

Psalm 62:7–8

Every day, demands are placed on our lives. Whether it is working at our job, raising our children, cooking for our family, making it to meetings and appointments on time, or cleaning our homes, certain things must get done every day. It is easy to feel like things will fall apart if we don't do things well or accomplish our tasks perfectly. Stress grows in our hearts. When this happens, it is a good thing to remember that our salvation depends on God and not on us.

Although we have many things to do every day, God is our strength, our refuge from the stressors and demands that require our attention. He is the one that we can run to, the one that we can rely on. Because of God's love for us, He will not forsake us or ignore us.

Have you had a hard day? Do you feel as if you are failing in life? "Pour out your heart" (62:8) to God before you sleep tonight. Tell Him how you feel and ask for His refreshing perspective on your life. Your salvation depends on Him, not on yourself. No matter what you do or don't do, God is the one who is taking care of you—every day. Fall asleep knowing that you are in His hands.

Flexing Your Joy Muscle

Today is a holy day for the Lord. Don't be sad because the joy you have in the Lord is your strength.

Nehemiah 8:10

When you stretch and strain your muscles, working them to the point of exhaustion, you can feel a "burn"—a painful but satisfying sensation guaranteeing that when the strained muscles heal, they will be bigger and stronger.

Just as temporary stress and strain ultimately produce strength in muscles, life's stresses and strains can ultimately result in spiritual strength. Even though it seems the weight of the world is almost unbearable, a heavenly hand wants to cup your elbow and help you lift the heavy burden. That's the joy of the Lord—a power source that is always available to give you the strength that you need.

Claim today as holy for the Lord, just as Nehemiah told the Israelites. The people had just heard the Word of the Lord read aloud and they were weeping as they realized how far they had strayed from God. That was a good thing, but Nehemiah didn't want them to weep, to feel guilty, to give up in depression. He challenged them to find joy in the God who still loved them and was drawing them back to Himself. He challenged them to let that joy give them strength to move forward, living as God wanted them to live.

God's joy will give you strength as well. Let the joy of the Lord flow through every part of you today as you and He carry your burdens together.

Never Forget

Praise the LORD, my soul! Praise his holy name, all that is within me. Praise the LORD, my soul, and never forget all the good he has done.

Psalm 103:1–2

We remember words of praise years after they are uttered. A timely "well-done" or some other pat on the back has the power to motivate you to do your best. Sometimes praise is all that keeps us going.

While God doesn't need praise, He is worthy of it all the same. With all that is within us, we are called to praise Him.

David, the ancient king of Israel and psalm writer, was known for his wholehearted worship of God. Through Psalm 103, he encourages his readers to "never forget all the good he has done." This isn't a Pollyanna notion uttered by a man who never suffered. This was a reality David lived while suffering.

As you prepare to sleep tonight, take five minutes to focus on the good things that the Lord has done for you today. Did He help you stay calm in a frustrating situation? Did He enable your child to finish an assignment well or learn a new skill? Did He provide food for your family's table? Did He bring sunshine in the middle of a cloudy day? If we look for God's presence in our day-to-day lives, we will surely see Him! Even the flowers growing outside that bring beauty to the earth are gifts from His hand—another thing for which we can praise Him. Then fall asleep with a smile on your face, knowing that God will be just as good tomorrow as He was today!

Tying Together

Almighty LORD, you made heaven and earth by your great strength and powerful arm. Nothing is too hard for you.

Jeremiah 32:17

It's too hard! There's no way I can do this! Do those thoughts ever reverberate through your mind?

Think back to when you were learning to tie your shoes. Your sweet chubby child's fingers were awkward as they tried to create that impossible bow. Time and time again you tried to imitate the adult who effortlessly, almost magically, created perfectly symmetrical bunny ears and ends of the right length out of nothing more than dangly strings.

Maybe you mastered "criss-cross applesauce" right away, but once past the bunny ears, everything seemed to fall apart. Frustration churned as you saw the result of your clumsy attempts. Perhaps you even declared defeat, vowing you'd wear Velcro shoes forever!

And yet, sweet friend, here you are today—able to tie your shoes! Continued practice coupled with a humble willingness to follow someone else's lead—someone who'd mastered the task—finally allowed you to reach your goal.

Now you have new goals. Are you caring for an aging parent? Is your chosen profession on hold? Is your marriage a daily struggle? Keep plugging away and follow the lead of the Master. Nothing is too hard for Him. Not one thing. Allow Him to work His mighty strength and power through precious, chosen you. Feel His agile hands guide your uneasy fingers as He helps you tie up your loose ends today.

The Changing Seasons

Those who cry while they plant will joyfully sing while they harvest. The person who goes out weeping, carrying his bag of seed, will come home singing, carrying his bundles of grain.

Psalm 126:5–6

Depending on where you live, a change in temperature marks a change in season. Trees change colors; certain crops are sown or harvested. Just as the seasons change, the seasons of our lives change, too. A change in circumstance or a shift in age can signal the change of a season of life.

There are difficult times in our lives when sorrow is heavy in our hearts and when joy seems to have disappeared from our days. These are seasons of tears. We lose a loved one, we fail, or we don't know how we will make it through another day. We seem to reap sorrow with every passing day.

But sorrow does not last forever. The image in this psalm is a beautiful one of hope. While the person who goes out in planting season is full of sorrow, he comes back from the fields in harvesting season "joyfully singing" as he brings in the bundles of grain. What made the difference? There's a clue in verse 3: "The Lord has done spectacular things for us. We are overjoyed." Seasons change.

If you are in a crying season, know that this season will not last forever. God understands the weariness of our hearts and walks with us through every circumstance. There will be a day, too, when you will joyfully sing again.

God's Daughter

Consider this: The Father has given us his love. He loves us so much that we are actually called God's dear children. And that's what we are.

1 John 3:1

Remember when life seemed uncomplicated? If you think back, you'll realize that a time once existed when a pretty red dress that billowed when you danced could make you the happiest little girl alive.

Where did those times go?

As much as those carefree days would be a welcome respite from the ups and downs of life today, it's also true that walking with God through the mountains and valleys of life has drawn you closer to Him. How much more do you know about Him because of where you've been together? How much more do you love Him because you've seen over and over how much He loves you?

This morning you continue your journey with your loving heavenly Father. You are a woman of God, but you are still His child—wide-eyed with wonder at His awesome presence and filled with joy at the truth of His promises. No matter what hurts or heartaches have come your way, your heavenly Father gathers you in His arms to comfort and strengthen you for the day ahead.

Yes, life is complex and complicated, but one simple truth cuts through all the static: You are a precious daughter of God.

Put on something red and rejoice in the love of your Father in heaven.

Patrolling in the Dark

Light will shine in the dark for a decent person. He is merciful, compassionate, and fair.

Psalm 112:4

When night falls with a cloak of darkness, we sometimes wonder what may be lurking in the shadows, especially if we're home alone. Sometimes noises around us sound threatening and dangerous when they're really just the rhythms of nature settling in for the night.

The doors are locked, the dog is snoring, but sleep won't come because you are on high alert against a threat—real or imagined. But remember, even though you may be surrounded by physical darkness, God's light of protection is shining brightly in and all around you. His is a light of compassion and mercy; He knows your fears and wants to illuminate the peace that is available to you for the asking.

Like a guard patrolling an important building, God keeps tabs on you. Any enemy against you has to emerge from the blackness into God's shimmering presence to get to you. These enemies include worries and fears. God's security sensor floodlights are set to turn on if an intruder crosses past them. He is your protector, so relax and trust the Lord with all the unknowns that remain in the dark.

Important Talk

Take to heart these words that I give you today. Repeat them to your children. Talk about them when you're at home or away, when you lie down or get up.

Deuteronomy 6:6–7

Ever heard the comment that women talk more than men? It's not politically correct these days to say it, but studies reveal that women consistently use more words in a day than men do.

Accept the way God designed you and enjoy the fact that talking to family and friends generally comes easy. However, it would be wise to distinguish between "just talking" and "important talk." In other words, those many words you use in a day should be more than just chatter. In fact, the command of Deuteronomy 6 is that some of those daily words should be from God's Word—His commands and promises repeated to those around us, at home or away, when lying down or getting up.

The verses specifically mention children, and if you're a mom, you know the importance of sharing God's Word with your kids. More than that, however, God gives you various places, people, and opportunities to share His words throughout your day, either as instruction or encouragement to others. As a friend, you may be the only one who encourages another woman today with the Word of God. "Like golden apples in silver settings, so is a word spoken at the right time" (Proverbs 25:11).

How will your words help your children today? Your husband? Your friends? Your co-workers? Ask that God take charge of the many words you will use today.

Take It Down a Notch

A gentle answer turns away rage, but a harsh word stirs up anger.

Proverbs 15:1

What happens when you add fuel to an already raging fire? It grows even hotter, doesn't it? Sometimes the fire rages out of control. Forests and houses go up in flames to the sadness of all.

The same is true with some of the responses we make to situations of conflict. When someone yells at you, what's your first response? To yell back? When we do that, we sometimes find our resentments magnified and our sleep troubled. Some arguments rage totally out of control and relationships are irreparably damaged.

When an angry mob of Ephraimites came to him with their grievances, Gideon, one of the Judges, took the time to soothe their resentment with a wise and humble answer (see Judges 8:1–3). He didn't allow exhaustion to spur him to answer in anger or in haste.

The writer of this proverb also knew the wisdom of giving a soft instead of a harsh answer. Instead of notching up the speed of emotions and tempers, a gentle answer takes it down a notch and helps to keep a matter from careening out of control. It defuses tempers and prevents wars.

Is there a matter you're struggling with? Perhaps someone made you angry and you're wondering how you will respond tomorrow. Take this time to pray. Ask the Lord to give you the wisdom and humility to provide "a gentle answer." Allow Him to take those feelings down a few notches and allow you to rest.

Never Alone

Be strong and courageous. Don't tremble! Don't be afraid of them! The LORD your God is the one who is going with you. He won't abandon you or leave you.

Deuteronomy 31:6

One of the largest but irrational fears of early childhood is abandonment. Little children don't realize they carry this fear, but it's behind some of their behavior and is especially evident when they go through separation anxiety.

Some adults still carry that fear. Perhaps as children, they were left behind in a school field trip, felt neglected by an emotionally absent parent, were ostracized by their peers, or were literally abandoned by those who should have cared for them. Those hard events make permanent impressions on the wet cement of the soul.

The good news is that God will never leave or forsake you. Nothing can separate you from His love. Did you wake this morning already burdened with a heavy load? Are you facing problems that you just don't know how to handle? Whatever you're facing, God knows. He surrounds you—His precious possession. He stands ready and able to provide love, assurance, wisdom, and help. You are not alone. You've never been alone.

This bright, new morning, revel in the fact that God is your all-knowing teacher, faithful friend, and loving parent. His enormous affection for you means He will never abandon or leave you. Today, believe in His protection and provision. Be strong and courageous. Step into your day knowing that "God is the one who is going with you."

Resting with the King

At night I remember your name, O LORD, and I follow your teachings.

Psalm 119:55

What do you find your mind dwelling on at night? The events of the day—good or bad? Words said or unsaid?

Consider the words of this short verse from the longest psalm in the Bible. In it, we are reminded that God is our Lord. It's a title of respect. In referring to God this way, we remember Him as the Ruler of the universe, the Supreme Being. He is the King of Kings (Revelation 17:14; 19:16).

Each of the titles for God can give us a quick glimpse into His role in our lives. It helps us understand how to relate to Him.

God is our Source.

He is our Salvation.

He is also our Comforter and Defender in times of need.

He is Mercy and Love.

When we remember His many titles, it becomes clear that He is here, on this very night, showing His great power as well as His compassion. It's good to recognize this as we prepare for sleep. The King is also our Father and we can trust deeply in Him.

As we prepare for this night of rest, we can call out "Lord" with awe and praise for the one who made everything. Then we recall His comforting presence. How kind He is to take our troubles and concerns into His hands! And if we ask, He'll give us guidance to be the best we can be tomorrow.

Soul Refreshment

Let my teachings come down like raindrops. Let my words drip like dew, like gentle rain on grass, like showers on green plants.

Deuteronomy 32:2

How refreshing is the Word of the Lord! The Father wants His Word to be soothing and nourishing. He wants His teachings to "come down like raindrops"—refreshing, cleansing, satisfying, just like your morning shower.

But sometimes it doesn't seem that way. You may at times feel that your devotions seem stale, your prayer time feels perfunctory, you're not feeling refreshed by God's Word at all. What can you do to enliven this time with God so that you come away feeling freshly showered? Perhaps it's a question of immersion. You don't get fully clean by sticking just your toe in the shower. You won't get the full effect of God's Word until you're immersed in it, until the teachings come down like raindrops around you.

God's Word is often compared to water, that most valuable and wholesome resource. Remember the blessed man that the psalmist praises in Psalm 1. The study of God's law, the Word of the Lord, makes this man "like a tree planted beside streams—a tree that produces fruit in season and whose leaves do not wither" (Psalm 1:3). The psalmist knows that a diligent study of the Word of God helps him produce fruit and keeps him from withering.

Remember that the Father wants His teachings to refresh you. Let today be one of the days when His Word is as soothing as "showers on green plants."

Look Up

Does your understanding make a bird of prey fly and spread its wings toward the south? Is it by your order that the eagle flies high and makes its nest on the heights? It perches for the night on a cliff. Its fortress is on a jagged peak.

Job 39:26–28

When life turns sour, we find ourselves reeling, trying to make sense of it all. Sometimes we look for someone to take responsibility for what's happened.

In a tailspin due to a series of tragedies in his life—the deaths of his children, the loss of his livestock, crops, and health—Job struggled to make sense of what God allowed. What had he done to cause God to allow such tragedy? He demands, "Let the Almighty answer me. Let the prosecutor write his complaint on a scroll" (Job 31:35).

Instead of justifying Himself, God instead asked Job a series of questions, the answers to which only God knew. God wanted to make Job look outside of himself and instead look to God. Job needed a merciful and all-powerful Savior.

With which areas of life do you struggle to trust the Lord? As you prepare for bed, look at the night sky and its dazzling stars. The Lord placed each of these tiny diamonds with precision. Think about the eagles on the cliffs, settling into their nests for the night. Worries and aspirations cannot move them. In the same meticulous way that Christ hung the stars and created all the creatures of the earth, He cares for His children. His loving vision for you is so much greater than your own. Release your grip on control with this knowledge and find rest.

Shine Brightly

May those who love the LORD be like the sun when it rises in all its brightness.

Judges 5:31

Watching the sun rise is a beautiful moment of the day. You feel privileged to see the sun emerge from behind the horizon, changing the landscape with its presence. Some sunrises are breathtaking. Vibrant colors spread across the sky, filling the morning with joy. Other sunrises are simple, without the explosions of color, but peaceful and calm. Both are beautiful in their own unique ways, for they usher in the promise of a new day. A sunrise reminds us of many of God's characteristics: His love for beauty, faithfulness which knows no end, and His grace that allows us to begin anew each day. The light of the sunrise points to our powerful, amazing God.

As the sun "rises in all its brightness," it shines on a waking world. Whether you can see the sunrise through your window or not, the image is beautiful. But even more important than the image is the spirit with which the author of this verse writes. The author is blessing you with these words, praying that you can be as remarkable and faithful as the sunrise.

As someone who cherishes the Lord, you can be like the rising sun, which inspires hope for the new day. You can be like the sunrise that points to God's beauty, faithfulness, and grace. And, like the sunrise, you can communicate God's warm love to the people in your world today.

My Comforter

Even when I am afraid, I still trust you. I praise the word of God. I trust God. I am not afraid. What can mere flesh and blood do to me?

Psalm 56:3–4

When you were a child, a stuffed animal or a blanket could eliminate nearly any apprehension or hurt, couldn't it? These comfort items, however, tend to lose their impact when suffering turns from the loss of a favorite toy to a grown-up variety: ailing family members, disagreeable bosses, and financial insecurity.

During the hard times of life, some seek comfort in relationships—spouses and other family members, close friends, etc. Others seek to escape or deaden the pain through less positive means: alcohol, drugs, meaningless relationships, workaholism. Yet the problems remain. Sometimes new problems emerge as a result.

David, the psalmist and famed giant killer, knew the source of ultimate comfort—God. In Psalm 56, David praises the Lord for His faithfulness and promises in the face of adversity. Having been hounded by taunting enemies for many years, David knew the peace of trusting God as his source of security. Unlike a person, God was never too busy to listen. And He had the power to conquer any enemy.

As you end this day, consider praising the Lord for His steadfastness and dependability during difficult moments. Make a list of the things that worry you. After each item, use the words of David and say to yourself, "I trust God." He alone is your comfort.

Firm Footing

God arms me with strength. His perfect way sets me free. He makes my feet like those of a deer and gives me sure footing on high places.

2 Samuel 22:33–34

Mountain goats are astonishing creatures. They prance around mountain ledges upon which any human would be frozen in terror. They scamper on cliffs high on a mountainside and seem to be perfectly comfortable in situations that, to us, appear dreadfully dangerous. God created mountain goats with feet that put our best climbing innovations to shame. Cloven in two and spread wide to increase balance, their hooves are also roughly padded, allowing their feet to maintain a grip on treacherous terrain.

Perhaps you are no stranger to a treacherous environment, a dangerous situation, a high place where you are very unsure of your footing. Perhaps that's the path that is set before you today. Even in this terrain, however, you can rejoice in the Lord: His promises are true. He is a shield that protects you. He is your rock, your strength, and your freedom.

As you walk your path today, remember that God promises the sure footing of the mountain goat so that you can balance on the high, dangerous places without a turned ankle, a stumble, or a slip. You can walk without fear of falling. Although you may look over the precipice and be filled with apprehension, turn your eyes back to the One who promises to never let you stumble or fall.

Two Choices

Turn all your anxiety over to God because he cares for you.
1 Peter 5:7

Wash your face, moisturize, brush and floss, set the alarm, turn all your anxiety over to God. It's just part of the bedtime routine. No problem, right?

Not so fast. It is much easier said than done. Is it any wonder that the subject of worry crops up time and time again in the Bible? The apostle Peter, who was with Jesus for three years, knew what his Master had to say about worry (see Matthew 6:25–34). Jesus made the point that worry doesn't add a single hour to your life and, in fact, shows lack of trust in God's promise to care for you. So Peter suggested that you take your anxiety and turn it over to God.

But how do you do that? Giving your worries to God is saying to Him, "I refuse to carry this worry because I know You already have the answer for me. I'm going to patiently wait for you to show it to me."

What is your day like when you're carrying worry? And how do you feel when you turn off the light? Dried up, exhausted. When you turn that anxiety over to God, however, you're able to flourish, to function, to move forward.

There will always be something to worry about. As you travel the road of life, you have two choices. Which side of the road do you want to be on—the side of anxiety and worry and deadness? or the side of life and health?

The answer is easy.

Waiting to Fly

Make your ways known to me, O LORD, and teach me your paths. Lead me in your truth and teach me because you are God, my savior. I wait all day long for you.

Psalm 25:4–5

When asking for directions, do you leave before you're given all the turns and signposts you need to watch for? When setting up new electronic equipment, do you read halfway through the instructions and then "wing it"—just hoping that you don't fry something when you turn it on? Of course not. Yet how often we lose patience when it comes to waiting for answers to prayer, how often we decide we're just going to wing it and hope for the best.

Answers to prayer do not often come immediately. Like the caterpillar in the chrysalis, waiting can be a long process. And yet, in your waiting, God will work in your heart in hidden ways. The beauty of the monarch's wings can only emerge after waiting for the right time. If the monarch emerges too soon, the wings will be spoiled and the butterfly will never fly.

Are you willing to believe that what God wants for you is far superior to anything that you could want for yourself? Are you willing to wait? While you wait God will grow you. While you wait He will meet you. While you wait you learn about sacrifice.

And how long must you wait? Does it really matter? God loves you. It is in this time of waiting that He will make His ways known to you, He will lead you in His truth, He will teach you.

That makes the waiting worthwhile.

You're Surrounded

*Elisha answered, "Don't be afraid. We have more forces on
our side than they have on theirs." . . . The LORD opened the
servant's eyes and let him see. The mountain around Elisha
was full of fiery horses and chariots.*

2 Kings 6:16–17

We love stories of bullies being defeated by the deserving un-
derdog. But in real life the stronger one—the one holding all the
power—wins, right? The bank manager who says no to your
request for a loan, that unreasonable boss who makes your life
or your spouse's life miserable, those who make our streets un-
safe—they seem to have the power. Troubles of the day seem to
have you surrounded as you try to sleep.

The Arameans—enemies of Israel—held the power in the
time of Elisha. After warning the king of Israel about the plans of
the Arameans, the king of Aram sent an army to capture Elisha.
While his servant panicked, Elisha prayed the prayer above. The
enemy may have had them surrounded. But God's army—one
much more powerful—had them surrounded too.

Today, consider what surrounds you. Perhaps you're facing
a wall of fears. Or, having contemplated a stack of unpaid bills,
unfinished projects, or unfriendly relationships in your life, you feel
totally alone, totally overwhelmed. But you are not in this alone.
Whether you are fighting to get all your work done, battling a serious
illness, or other threats to your peace, He is with you. His heavenly
army and His powerful love surround you like a warm embrace.

As you slip under the covers, bask in the knowledge that a
far more powerful ally fights for you.

Commanding Voices

Entrust your ways to the Lord. Trust him, and he will act on your behalf. He will make your righteousness shine like a light, your just cause like the noonday sun.

Psalm 37:5–6

Sometimes you may get the feeling that everyone has ideas for your life: do this activity, try that product, become this kind of a woman. These suggestions bombard you from all sides. Try as hard as you may, you can never follow all of these commands. What's more, you will never be happy listening to all of these voices that tell you conflicting things to do.

At your first reading of these verses, you might think the author is just as bossy as the people of this world. After all, the author commands you to do many things, all listed in a very short space! You are told to trust the Lord, do good things, live in the land, practice being faithful, be happy with the Lord, and entrust your ways to Him. It's almost as overwhelming as flipping through a magazine, looking only at the advertisements and self-help articles. But when you look at the passage again, the commands the author exhorts you to obey are encouraging and affirming. Why? Because when you trust in Him, He "will give you the desires of your heart," "will act on your behalf," and "will make your righteousness shine like a light, your just cause like the noonday sun."

When you trust the Lord and do good, you become a bright light in a dark world.

Soak It In

Rather, he delights in the teachings of the LORD and reflects on his teachings day and night.

Psalm 1:2

If there is a tree outside your bedroom window, take a minute to gaze at it. Consider its height and width.

A tree gains water and nourishment from the soil. The xylem of a tree—the cells that form the rings of a tree—enable the tree to take water out of the soil and therefore "feed" the leaves. A tree has to continually take in water to refresh its leaves. If the tree didn't take in water, the leaves would wither.

The same is true for us. While we understand the need for proper hydration, sometimes we forget to "hydrate" through the Word. Busy schedules, problems, and other obstacles keep our spiritual xylems from soaking in refreshment. Instead, we're bombarded by images and words that don't help us to grow.

In describing how a godly person "is like a tree planted beside streams—a tree that produces fruit in season and whose leaves do not wither" (Psalm 1:3), the writer of Psalm 1 described the strategy of this person: "he delights in the teachings of the LORD and reflects on his teachings day and night."

Tonight He speaks peace into your soul. He delights to fill you with His love and wisdom from His Word. After reading, close your eyes and reflect on God's truths, goodness, and faithfulness. Then take a second look at the tree outside the window. You are like that tree—fed by God's Word, growing tall in God's grace.

Sunrise, Sunset

Those who live at the ends of the earth are in awe of your miraculous signs. The lands of the morning sunrise and evening sunset sing joyfully.

Psalm 65:8

An elderly man once remarked that when he woke each morning, he checked to see which side of the sod he was on and found it miraculous that he was still on the top.

How do you respond to the arrival of each new morning? Are you amazed by each new day you've been granted or do you roll over, hit the snooze button, and growl at anyone or anything that disturbs you?

Wherever you are, you are living in a miracle. Think about it: When the sun is rising for you, it is setting for those on the opposite side of the globe. The wondrous sunrise you experience is a sunset for someone else, thousands of miles away. How many people are, all at once, gazing in awe at the miracle of one day, both beginning and ending?

And, in the midst of the millions who praise Him, God cares for you. He knows your name and hears your prayers!

Puts things into perspective, doesn't it? Rather than just checking the sod, make a point of praising God for something new each day. Look out your window and allow yourself to be awed by His creation. Don't just hit the snooze button! Find joy in this morning's sunrise, and be thankful for the gift of another day to live for Him.

A Silver Lining

Turn to me, and have pity on me. I am lonely and oppressed.
Relieve my troubled heart, and bring me out of my distress.

Psalm 25:16–17

Some days are easier to get through than others. Perhaps today you were reminded of how alone you feel with no one with which to share your struggles. It's like a dark cloud hanging over you. Even with a loving family, you can still feel alone as you contemplate problems or issues demanding a response from you. Such feelings are often magnified at night as the darkness closes in. You want to run, but there seems nowhere to go. You want to scream, but there is no one to hear. You want to pray, but wonder if God is listening.

David, the psalmist, could relate. His psalms contain some of the most gut-wrenching cries for help that you'll find in the Bible. This one is no exception. Though surrounded by the dark clouds of loneliness and oppression, David didn't hold back his pain. Instead, he grasped for the silver lining in the cloud by unabashedly calling out for God to rescue him.

You've heard the old saying, "Every cloud has a silver lining." Perhaps you see only the darkness of the cloud at this moment. Yet there is a silver lining on the horizon.

God is there. Cry out to Him tonight. Share the full weight of your discouragement or pain with Him. Ask Him to not only help you rest tonight, but rest in the knowledge that He is looking out for you.

Calling Your Name

Do not be afraid, because I have reclaimed you. I have called you by name; you are mine. When you go through the sea, I am with you. When you go through rivers, they will not sweep you away.

Isaiah 43:1–2

This morning, the Lord reminds you: "I have called you by name; you are mine." Let your unsettled heart be calmed, let your fears and loneliness cease. He whispers to you, His daughter, "Do not be afraid, because I have reclaimed you." You were His once, but you were torn apart in sin from Him. But He has brought you back to Himself because of His great love—"I have reclaimed you," He says, "you are mine."

What precious promises—that the God of the universe would reach down to touch your soul this morning with His reminder of how much you mean to Him. And beyond that, He promises never to leave you, never to let you face difficulty alone. The trials of life will come, but He will be with you. When you go through the storms on the sea, battered by circumstances and worry, He is with you, protecting you, holding you above the threatening waves to keep you from going under. When the river's current makes you afraid that you'll never be able to stand without being knocked over, He will hold you close and keep you from being swept away. When you must walk through the scathing fire of criticism, anger, or pain, you will emerge without burns, without harm.

Whether you're facing a raging sea, a swift-flowing river, or a scorching fire, God places your hand in His and says, "I am with you. We can walk through this together."

My Feet Are Slipping

*When I said, "My feet are slipping," your mercy, O LORD,
continued to hold me up. When I worried about many things,
your assuring words soothed my soul.*

Psalm 94:18–19

Gymnastics is a precision sport combining tumbling and acrobatic
feats. Is there anything more exciting than seeing a gymnast not
only walk across but do a series of handsprings or a handstand
on a narrow balance beam?

Life can sometimes seem like a balancing act—one no less
compelling than that of a gymnast. On some days, you might feel
extremely competent at balancing work and family schedules,
household tasks, and other demands. But on other days, perhaps
you feel as if your feet keep slipping on that balance beam as more
demands pile up than you feel capable of meeting.

Perhaps tonight you're wondering how you can please
everyone or get everything done. Or perhaps you're mourning
the fact that you fell off the beam, as it were, and pleased no
one—including yourself.

The writer of Psalm 94 has the perfect response for anxious
times like this: call out for help. His words show the kind of SOS
call that always gets God's attention.

Like the psalmist, although you may feel your feet are slipping, God will hold you up. His assuring words will soothe, and
His mighty hand can sustain you through the acrobatic ventures
you may face tomorrow.

A Light to Live By

The sun will no longer be your light during the day, nor will the brightness of the moon give you light, but the LORD will be your everlasting light. Your God will be your glory.

Isaiah 60:19

Sundials are both beautiful and fascinating. They appear almost like works of art—designed with precision and strategically placed in lush surroundings such as a garden full of sunlight. You probably have never needed to master the art of telling time on a sundial, but you know the basics: The sun casts a shadow from the centerpiece onto the dial where someone skilled could discern a general time of the day. As the earth turned and the sun swept across the sky, the shadow moved around the dial.

Most sundials today are simply placed for looks since most people use more modern methods of time-telling. However, the world still depends on the regularity of the sun to order its days. Plant life, animal life, people, and all of nature count on the movements of the sun and the moon to regulate our time, to move the tides, to change the seasons.

There will be a time, though, when the sun and the moon will no longer shine. No longer will they dictate when you rise and when you sleep. At one point in the future, the Lord will literally become your "everlasting light."

As the sun rises this morning, thank the Lord that He promises to be the source of everlasting light through all eternity. Thank Him that today He is your spiritual light—nourishing you, warming you, guiding you.

Guiding Light

*By day the LORD went ahead of them in a column of smoke to lead
them on their way. By night he went ahead of them in a column of
fire to give them light so that they could travel by day or by night.*

Exodus 13:21

If you've ever driven on a dark, foggy night, you know the welcome relief of seeing red taillights ahead of you along the road. There's a certain level of comfort in knowing that you're not alone in the fog, that someone else is driving carefully along and you can stay close and follow.

Some situations in life are just as murky. Unresolved issues in relationships, tasks without clear direction, or multiple opportunities can cause confusion and stress. At those times, we need clear guidance by which to navigate and avoid trouble.

When the people of Israel left Egypt, they probably weren't sure how they were going to get from Point A to Point B—the Promised Land. So the Lord went before them "in a column of smoke" during the day and "a column of fire" at night. These were visible symbols of His presence and His commitment to guide them to the Promised Land. Best of all, God never led them faster than their ability to travel.

In need of guidance? As the passage above shows, God is more than capable of providing it in many forms. He may send a friend with timely advice or provide just the right Scripture to illuminate your situation. He also provides the warmth of His presence through the special smile or hug of a spouse. Like those welcome red taillights, God is guiding and you can safely follow. You can rest assured tonight knowing that the Guiding Light goes before you.

Stormy Weather

I know the plans that I have for you, declares the LORD. They are plans for peace and not disaster, plans to give you a future filled with hope. Then you will call to me. You will come and pray to me, and I will hear you.

Jeremiah 29:11–12

Open your calendar or your pocket planner and take a look at today's schedule. What activities crowd your day? Scan the next few weeks or months. Chances are you have plans jotted in—an appointment here, a meeting there, a vacation week penciled in over here. Your life is neatly planned out and you pretty much know what to expect out of today and the coming days.

But what do you do when your neatly planned schedule gets blown off course? The unexpected stormy wind whips through your planned-out sunny day. You catch a bad sickness and end up in bed for a few days; a family member needs your help; a sudden turn of events takes your life and turns it upside down.

Even though you might enjoy a change from your routine once in a while, you probably don't relish sudden, life-altering events. But, as you can probably attest, these things happen. When faced with these unexpected storms, you can be assured that God already has the way planned for you. He knows what today will bring, whether that particular event is on your schedule or not.

God's plans for you are the best. As He told Jeremiah, His plans are for peace, not disaster. His plans are to give you a future filled with hope. So when your days are sunny, cloudless, and go exactly as planned, give thanks. And when the unexpected storm arrives, handle it gracefully, and thank God that He is in control.

A Protective Shield

I lie down and sleep. I wake up again because the LORD continues to support me.

Psalm 3:5

The day is over. Or is it? Perhaps you take to bed unmet expectations, frustrations, and fears of the day. Worries wash over you like waves pounding against a shore. You feel alone and unsupported as you consider what has been done or needs to be done.

At the time King David wrote this psalm, he was running from his son Absalom, who rebelled against him and tried to take over his throne. Imagine the stress of having a family member turn against you. (Perhaps you don't have to imagine this.) Yet David was confident in the Lord's protection while he slept. As he explained in another part of the psalm, "But you, O LORD, are a shield that surrounds me. You are my glory. You hold my head high" (3:3).

God is the same for us—a protective shield from harm and fear, stronger than any enemy we face. We can sleep without fear or worry knowing that He supports us.

Every day that we wake up again is because of the Lord's continual protection and presence in our lives. As you climb into bed tonight, reflect on the ways God supported you throughout the day. Then, fall asleep knowing that He will continue to protect you.

Fruit of the Vine

Live in me, and I will live in you. A branch cannot produce any fruit by itself. It has to stay attached to the vine. In the same way, you cannot produce fruit unless you live in me.

John 15:4

You're ambling along a vineyard, swinging a basket and peering among the branches for the ripest, plumpest fruit. Many grapes are still greenish so you leave them to mature. But then you spy a particularly bountiful area and move in, anticipating the delightful thump of each cluster as it lands in your basket. You can't help but sample one savory specimen and as the juice bursts onto your tongue, you appreciate the gift of fruit ripened to perfection in its due season.

Squatting to reach a low cluster, however, you notice a branch that has snapped, perhaps by a violent wind. What a shame, you think, noticing that what once held so much potential now yields only dead fruit, brown and shriveled, that will benefit no one. Being cut off from its supply of life-giving sustenance, the branch has withered and died, no longer able to do what it was created to do.

Do you ever feel like that dried-up branch? Jesus clearly teaches that apart from Him all labor is in vain. If you want a life that bears lasting fruit, you must stay connected to Him, your life source.

At the joint where branch meets vine, there's a lovely co-mingling of your humanity and His supernatural divinity; they coalesce to give birth to beautiful fruit just dripping with His sweet goodness—today and every day for the rest of your life.

The Temple of the Lord

Night and day may your eyes be on this temple, the place about which you said, "My name will be there." Listen to me as I pray toward this place.

1 Kings 8:29

You may have had conversations where you're certain that the person you're talking to isn't really listening. Sometimes we think of prayer in the same way. Even as we pour out our hearts, we wonder if God is listening to us, or if we are only praying to the ceiling. Ever think that?

After the completion of Israel's first temple, King Solomon prayed during the dedication. Knowing that God's presence would fill the temple, Solomon asked God to listen to his prayers and trusted that God would not ignore him.

What thoughts are on your mind tonight? What hopes or concerns are in your heart? If you believe in Jesus, you are filled with His Holy Spirit and have become the new temple of God. You are treasured by the Father who loves you. As the apostle Peter explained, "The Lord's eyes are on those who do what he approves. His ears hear their prayer" (1 Peter 3:12).

As you prepare for sleep, remember that God's eyes are on you and His ears are open to your prayer. You are not praying to the ceiling. So tell Him what's on your mind this night—He is ready and willing to listen.

God's Temple

Don't you know that you are God's temple and that God's Spirit lives in you?

1 Corinthians 3:16

Solomon built one. Zerubbabel built one. You are one—a living temple fashioned and crafted by God Himself. Ancient temples used gold, silver, and precious metals as symbols of purity and holiness; they were places people believed their gods lived. Solomon's magnificent temple (read about it in 1 Kings 6) and Zerubbabel's temple (a rebuilding of Solomon's temple after its destruction by the Babylonians—see 2 Kings 25 and Ezra 3) were places for God's presence among His people. However, with Christ came a new living temple made of people who believe in Him and who are made beautiful by the presence of the Holy Spirit within each one.

Maybe this morning you don't feel like a beautiful temple of God. The past casts shadows around every nook and cranny—whether from bad choices, poor decisions, or costly mistakes. Seasons of neglect or strife have caused crumbling walls or a cracking foundation.

No matter what you have built in your life before, today is a new day! A day to be renewed and encouraged, knowing that the Holy Spirit is there with you, beside you, in you. He is ready and waiting to be your source of strength and hope this day, especially in the middle of your challenges. Choose today to be a living temple founded on Christ and transformed by the Holy Spirit—a place of character where God resides, a place of beauty where God is reflected, a place of sanctuary where God is welcomed.

Wrestling in the Night

So Jacob was left alone. Then a man wrestled with him until dawn.

Genesis 32:24

So often, we wrestle with God about what is happening in our lives. And nighttime is usually when that wrestling happens. In the dark, fears and questions easily rise to the surface of our hearts.

As Jacob traveled back to his homeland to meet Esau, many fears probably rose to his heart. After all, he stole his brother Esau's birthright and deceived their father. He was not certain what type of homecoming he could expect. But just before he met Esau, he encountered a strange man who "wrestled with him until dawn" (verse 24). Neither would let the other go, and even after the man dislocated his hip, Jacob refused to stop fighting until he received a blessing.

Jacob realized that he was not wrestling against a mere man but against God (verse 30). And God was gracious to him. He received not only a blessing, but a new name: Israel, which means "He Struggles With God" (verse 28).

It is okay to "wrestle" with God—to ask Him difficult questions and cry out to Him for help and mercy. Because of Christ's death and resurrection, you are loved by God and can go "confidently to the throne of God's kindness to receive mercy and find kindness, which will help us at the right time" (Hebrews 4:16). He is the God who blesses His people. Tonight, whatever you are wrestling with God about, ask Him for His blessing, and for a new start.

Bask in the Task

*So, whether you eat or drink, or whatever you do, do everything
to the glory of God.*

1 Corinthians 10:31

Rolling out of bed this morning, did your task list infiltrate your
thoughts? Did it cross your mind what a drag it can be just keeping
up with the daily grind? It's so easy to feel caught in a rut since
the details of life can seem menial and sometimes meaningless.

But God desires joy for you amidst those ruts. In fact, you can
bring Him glory there. As today's verse indicates, what you do
sometimes matters much less to God than how you do it.

Anyone can wipe down the kitchen for the third time in one
day, but not everyone can do it while rockin' a praise song.

Anyone can re-do a project at work because the boss gave
the wrong instructions the first time, but not everyone can do it
without grumbling.

Anyone can go elbow deep in the toilet to work on a rust
stain, but many aren't willing to do it at all, much less happily.

As undignified or "un-fun" as some tasks seem, they can
bring glory to God if you approach them with a servant's heart.
Remember Jesus illustrating this to the disciples by washing their
filthy feet? And yet He was happy to do it.

Now you—purposefully chosen you—are being used to bless
others who might not even show appreciation. But dear one, rest
assured: There's One beaming down at you, pleased at your willingness to do all things for His glory. Can you feel His pleasure?

You'll Be Complete

I'm convinced that God, who began this good work in you,
will carry it through to completion on the day of Christ Jesus.

Philippians 1:6

Sometimes we go to bed at night frustrated at the tasks on our "to-do" lists that are now on our "not done" lists. Many times we create lists for ourselves that are impossible to finish, or the interruptions of other activities took up the time we thought we'd have to check off the tasks on our lists.

What a relief to know that the Lord never leaves anything undone. He finishes the job at hand. That includes the work He has begun in you. When you decided to become a follower of Christ, God began changing your heart and your life. Just like any other important project, a great deal of effort and thought are being devoted to "finishing" you. Like a craftsman who carves away at a block of wood, He patiently works a piece at a time—carving here, finely sanding there.

God is a Master Craftsman, working on your life. He alone sees the finished product—and so every chip, every cut, every fine bit of sanding is creating an object of perfection.

You many not have completed everything you set out to do today, but rest assured that your list will be there tomorrow. Tonight, thank the Master Craftsman for His continued patient work with you. Remember that quality workmanship takes time and intricate crafting. You will one day be a completed work of exquisite design because God always finishes what He starts.

Rooted in Love

*I also pray that love may be the ground into which you sink
your roots and on which you have your foundation. This way,
with all of God's people you will be able to understand how
wide, long, high, and deep his love is.*

Ephesians 3:17–18

When the apostle Paul wanted to describe believers' relationship
with God, he drew upon the powerful image of roots sunk deep
into the ground. A magnificent tree stands tall only because of a
deep and wide root system that provides a strong solid foundation
against the storms as well as nourishment from deep in the soil.

The metaphor of the roots beautifully portrays the relationship
you should have with the love of Christ: Christ's love holds you
fast in the midst of storms and nourishes you constantly. Like a
tree, you can choose to be constantly sinking the roots of your
life into Christ's foundational love. The deeper you root yourself
in Him, the less likely you will be upturned by life's storms. By
being rooted in Christ's love, you will find yourself filled with
God. You will begin to understand "how wide, long, high, and
deep his love is." You find that it surrounds you—you can't get
over it, around it, under it, or through it. His love is a hedge
around you in ways that go beyond your ability to understand.
And the more you learn about Christ's love, the more you become
filled up with Him.

Like a tree standing tall in the forest, send your roots deep into
Christ's love. Ask Him to fill you up today with His amazing love.

Nothing Can Separate

Nothing can ever separate us from God's love which Christ Jesus our Lord shows us.

Romans 8:38

When we've blown it, we can't help rehashing the incident over and over in our minds. We fervently wish that we had a "do-over"—a way to undo what was done.

Perhaps today you made some choices or said something that you feel will keep you from God. The fact that it's too late to unsay or undo what was done robs you of sleep. If so, the apostle Paul has good news: nothing in creation can separate you from the love God has for you.

As humans, our love is often based on certain conditions being met. When they aren't, our love grows cold. But God's love is unconditional—no strings are attached. It is the most powerful force in history. By the power of His love, mountains have moved, seas have parted, and very old women have given birth to healthy babies. That's the kind of love that flows over you tonight. Because of His love, there is nothing that divides us and God. His love bridges any gap.

God loves you not because of your behavior, choices, or talents but because of who you are in Him. Rest your weary head on His shoulder and let His love fill your heart tonight. Nothing can keep you apart from Him.

Songs in the Heart

Let Christ's word with all its wisdom and richness live in you. Use psalms, hymns, and spiritual songs to teach and instruct yourselves about God's kindness. Sing to God in your hearts.

Colossians 3:16

Songs have a remarkable way of filling our minds. Melodies meander around the edge of your subconscious while you go about your day. They repeat endlessly, permeating your thoughts with catchy choruses, clever snippets, and melodic tunes. You can be concentrating on other things when suddenly a line comes out of your mouth. This is potentially embarrassing (especially around strangers), but the embarrassment doesn't stop the song reverberating through your head.

It's no wonder, then, that you are encouraged to let Christ's word live in you through songs. And better to sing a song endlessly than to let your heart grow downtrodden. Worshiping through song can be a powerful connection with God. The apostle Paul encouraged the Colossian believers to have "psalms, hymns, and spiritual songs" ringing through their heads, sticking in their minds with tenacity, for along with those melodies would come Christ's word in all its wisdom and richness. Singing to God in your head will certainly carry over to your heart, allowing God to have an active presence in your life. As you sing the songs in your heart throughout the day, you will have God's kindness and wisdom dwelling in you.

So don't be afraid to sing! Your best audience is God, and He loves to hear you!

Mind-Boggling Goodness

As Scripture says: "No eye has seen, no ear has heard, and no mind has imagined the things that God has prepared for those who love him."

1 Corinthians 2:9

What would be the most amazing thing that could happen to you in your life? Winning the lottery? Getting a 200 percent raise increase at work just because? Your husband telling you to take a week's vacation at a spa by yourself—he'll take care of the kids? Mister Perfect showing up at your doorstep tomorrow with arms full of long-stemmed red roses and a marriage proposal? A well-known TV program calling to say that your home has been selected for a million-dollar makeover? Your favorite sports team winning the national championship two years in a row?

Sometimes it's nice to dream big about our lives on earth. But we can also dream big about eternity. Perhaps you've wondered what heaven will be like. We've heard of pearly gates, streets of gold, no more crying, our own mansions, no more fear, pain, or death. Yet even with that description the Bible promises that heaven will blow our minds. Not even the wisest, the most educated, not even the greatest theologian has even an inkling of what God has prepared for those who love Him.

Tonight, as you pray, you ask God to renew your sense of wonder in the things He's promised to do for you. Pray for a sense of expectation, to not get so caught up in the mundane details of life that you forget that there's something mind-bogglingly better waiting for you. Thank Him for giving you the chance to dream.

His Presence in Presents

Every good present and every perfect gift comes from above, from the Father who made the sun, moon, and stars. The Father doesn't change like the shifting shadows produced by the sun and the moon.

James 1:17

Think back to your birthdays when you were a little girl. Can you remember trying to harness your anticipation until you thought you were going to burst? You knew that those beautifully wrapped presents had been chosen carefully just for you and when you were finally allowed to tear into the wrapping paper, you were overjoyed at what was inside! There were some items from your list as well as some better-than-imagined surprises. Your parents knew how to delight their precious daughter.

And so does Someone else. Just think how even more perfect the gifts are that God showers on you. Matthew 7:11 says, "Even though you're evil, you know how to give good gifts to your children. So how much more will your Father in heaven give good things to those who ask him?" He provides every good and perfect gift and His desire to do so never changes.

What presents has God already given you? Imagine Him happily planning the details of surprising you with them, smiling at your reaction. And He's not finished yet! Begin to look forward to—just as you did during those childhood birthdays—what He has in store for you, His precious daughter. As you spend today with your heavenly Father, allow yourself to get lost in the giddiness of anticipating what perfect gift He's wrapping up just for you.

Puzzling over His Plans

Just as the heavens are higher than the earth, so my ways are higher than your ways, and my thoughts are higher than your thoughts.

Isaiah 55:9

We like being on the same page with someone—having a common understanding. But have you ever been in a conversation with someone and found yourself puzzling over something that was said? Many conflicts begin with a misunderstanding and continue with resentment or lack of trust.

We sometimes misunderstand God because we're uncertain of His ways. We think we have God figured out even when we sometimes lack a crucial piece of the puzzle: His input. Therefore we might limit what He could do or assume that He would do exactly what we might do in a circumstance.

In a prophecy for the exiles who would someday return to Palestine after years of captivity, God spoke through the prophet Isaiah concerning His inscrutable ways. Instead of writing off His rebellious people, God promised to show them mercy. All they had to do was return to Him. When they did, He promised to totally forget their wrong (Psalm 103:12; Isaiah 43:25).

If you're feeling yourself at an emotional distance from God due to regret or guilt, consider returning to Him. God holds all of the pieces to the puzzle. He turns mishaps and misfortunes into kingdom builders. Relax in the knowledge that He is up to something spectacular in your life!

Ticktock

Dear friends, don't ignore this fact: One day with the Lord is like a thousand years, and a thousand years are like one day.

2 Peter 3:8

Hollywood does a good job of making time travel seem extraordinarily commonplace. Whether riding in a DeLorean or stepping through a wardrobe, people have been able to travel in time—for better or for worse.

In these verses, Peter is not spilling the cosmic secret to altering the space-time continuum. Rather, he's giving a glimpse of the infinite and eternal God. Because He has always existed and always will exist, time itself means very little to Him. Because you are on this earth for only a limited amount of time, however, every minute counts. You live your life by the clock—there is a time when you arise in the morning, times when you eat, work, play, exercise, do your devotions, go to church, go to bed . . .

So you might wonder, what is it all for, anyway, this daily routine which recycles every twenty-four hours? Why can't Jesus return as He promised and take you to be with Him in heaven, ending this boring, merry-go-round existence?

The answer is in verse 9: He is being patient, allowing others the opportunity to repent and come to know Him, just as you know Him.

So when you wake up and the cycle begins again, rejoice. Pray for those whom you might influence today for Christ. Think of those who will come to salvation this very day. After all, that is the only reason the cycle continues.

More than Sparrows

Aren't two sparrows sold for a penny? Not one of them will fall to the ground without your Father's permission. Every hair on your head has been counted. Don't be afraid! You are worth more than many sparrows.

Matthew 10:29–31

Even if we have the veneer of "having it all together," we can sometimes feel worthless. Illnesses that rob us of strength or cause hair loss; problems in families; financial reversals—these can all eat away at our confidence and leave us wondering what tomorrow will bring.

Through the words of Jesus as recorded in the Gospel of Matthew, God reminds you that you are worth more than many sparrows. There are many different types of sparrows: House, American tree, Eurasian tree, Savannah, Black-throated, White-throated—the list continues. They are small and seemingly insignificant to some and are a nuisance to others. In Jesus' time, two could be sold for very little. However, the God of the universe always knows if they falter, fly, or fall. If He tends to the needs of these small brown birds, you can rest tonight knowing He will notice every detail of your life.

Take your fears to the Lord every moment of the day. He knows every inch of your body, having formed you in your mother's womb (Psalm 139:13–14). Just as He knows the number of hairs on your head, He knows your struggles and joys. God doesn't want you to be fearful, but trusting. Hear Him whisper tonight, "Don't be afraid! You are worth more than many sparrows."

Cleansing Confession

God is faithful and reliable. If we confess our sins, he forgives them and cleanses us from everything we've done wrong.

1 John 1:9

Confessing your sins is probably not the first thing that springs to mind as you roll out of bed in the morning. You may automatically turn on the coffeepot, or maybe throw on clothes to exercise. But confessing your sins? That may seem like more of an end-of-the-day ritual, something to do after you've snapped at a family member, complained about a co-worker, or yearned after someone else's possessions.

In the morning, however, you may see more clearly some of the events of yesterday that cause you to wince into your coffee cup this morning. You may see your anxiety, your anger, or your selfishness more clearly when given the perspective of this new morning. While it's not good to dwell on the past, if you do find issues that need some cleansing—before God and perhaps before someone you may have wronged—then now is the time to do it. Ask for God's forgiveness and make a plan to ask that person's forgiveness if needed.

As you ask for forgiveness, take comfort in this promise that God is faithful and reliable to cleanse you from everything you've done wrong. Like cleansing water, He will wash away your sins, just as He has every other time. He will cleanse you from everything you've done wrong. He will give you the strength to avoid repeating that sin in this new day.

Confess and refresh. Now that's something to smile about!

An Amazing Language

At the same time the Spirit also helps us in our weakness, because we don't know how to pray for what we need. But the Spirit intercedes along with our groans that cannot be expressed in words.

Romans 8:26

No one understands why dolphins protect humans, but stories of them rescuing humans go back to ancient Greece. Many of the cited cases portray a person swimming in the ocean in harm's way of a shark when dolphins come to the rescue. It leaves you wondering how they communicate the need to help this victim.

Dolphins have an amazing language all their own. It's made up of squeaks, whistles, and clicks. Although we cannot hear nor understand them, they understand each other. Their communication patterns have helped save many humans from danger.

Today, perhaps you've felt as if predators lurked all around. Tonight, you cry out in your weakness not knowing what to say. You know you need to pray, but words won't come. You want to communicate your needs, but you're left speechless. There are no words—just sighs, moans, and whimpers.

Just as the dolphins communicate in a language you cannot understand, so does the Spirit of God. He hears your moans and takes them before the throne of God. Our garbled communication becomes intelligible in His capable hands.

Tonight, know that your moans are heard. Know your groans are turned into words through the Spirit. He intercedes for you, even when you don't know what to pray. It's an amazing language. He's an amazing God.

Help Is on the Way

There's no one like your God, Jeshurun! He rides through the heavens to help you. In majesty he rides through the clouds.

Deuteronomy 33:26

Your phone rings. A good friend who recently moved cross-country is on the line. She is in the midst of a serious family health crisis and needs practical help: childcare, household assistance, meals. She doesn't yet know anyone in her town, and she's overwhelmed with all that must be done to keep her household running over the next several days.

More than anything, you want to be there to help, but your own family or job responsibilities keep you tethered in your current location. Though you know your friend appreciates your support and your commitment to intercede for her family, you wish you could do more.

You wish you could be there.

Moses wanted his people to know that when they needed help, they could call on God and He would come to their aid. His words portray a rescuer racing across time and space to provide the help they needed. Moses used the term "Jeshurun" here, a term of affection for Israel. He wanted his beloved nation to know that God would be there. All they had to do was ask and He would ride across the heavens and through the clouds to get to them.

Our unchanging God is there for each one of us who calls Him Lord. No matter whether it is the need of your distant friend, or a need much closer to home in your own life, God's help is on the way.

Take Me Away

Be angry without sinning. Don't go to bed angry.
Ephesians 4:26

Tonight, perhaps you find yourself quoting the famous bubble-bath advertising slogan, "Calgon, take me away!" But what sparked the need? Opposition from a family member? Tension because of an unresolved issue? Wouldn't it be great if climbing into a luxurious hot bubble bath with candles surrounding the tub permanently took away the problems of the day? We'd be there all day if that were true!

Hanging on to the incident will only cause the anger to grow to a level where it affects everything you do. It is so easy to hang on to your anger, frustrations, and wrongs. But soon you realize it is those you love the most who suffer if you are unwilling to surrender.

Want to really escape? Follow the advice of the apostle Paul. Do whatever it takes to resolve the issue. He follows up the advice above with a good reason for resolution: "Don't give the devil any opportunity to work" (Ephesians 4:27). Not wanting to give the evil one any traction, you make a conscious decision to forget, to forgive, and to make the wrong right.

By following Paul's advice, you can feel God's pure delight pouring over you as your soul unwinds. A heavenly "Calgon" moment of surrender helps take away the anger and soothe the soul.

A Spotless Light

Aaron must burn sweet-smelling incense on this altar every morning when he takes care of the lamps.

Exodus 30:7

In the early 1900s, people used oil lamps with round glass globes to provide light for a dark room. When the glass became blackened from smoke, the globe would be carefully removed and the soot wiped off. This cleaning became almost a daily routine. Every morning they had a choice whether to clean their lamp or wait until later. If cleaning was postponed, the light would grow dim, and the lamp would be useless in the nighttime.

Notice that as the worship at the tabernacle was instituted, God told Moses that Aaron was to take care of the lamps every morning, rather than only once a week or every other week. Everything having to do with worship at the tabernacle had to be done according to God's specifics. None of the rituals could be neglected. So Aaron would have to be disciplined about maintaining the lamps.

The oil lamp can be a metaphor for life. How can you keep your lamp clean and maintain a sweet-smelling relationship with the Lord? While God will provide the cleansing, it's up to us to ask Him to reveal and wash away any sin in our lives.

Determine how you can be a spotless light for the Lord that shines brilliantly in the darkness around you. Go to God this morning and let Him wipe off any darkness that has accumulated so you can be a light before Him today.

Smile!

Always be joyful. Never stop praying. Whatever happens, give thanks, because it is God's will in Christ Jesus that you do this.

1 Thessalonians 5:16–18

When was the last time someone told you to "put a smile on your face"? Following that piece of advice is the last thing you want to do when you're in pain. Yet perhaps you know people who take this advice to heart out of a conviction that faking an emotion is better than showing the world how they really feel. Is that something you believe?

The apostle Paul was not advocating faking an emotion as he wrote to the believers of Thessalonica. Instead, he advised his readers to "always be joyful." While such a sentiment sounds impossible in the face of some of life's tragedies, consider the fact that being joyful doesn't mean hiding behind a plastered smile on your face. It means that you know where your hope and joy ultimately lie—with the Lord. Only the Holy Spirit can help you to "always be joyful" or to "give thanks" even when life is at its most difficult.

The more you realize your blessings, the more you understand how to be joyful always. As you snuggle up in bed tonight, make a mental list of some of these blessings. Perhaps this litany of blessings will help put a smile on your face as you drift off to sleep.

Life in Motion

Early in the morning Hezekiah gathered the leaders of the city and went to the LORD's temple.

2 Chronicles 29:20

Do you remember learning about the principle of inertia in science class? An object at rest tends to remain at rest; an object in motion tends to remain in motion. It takes an applied force greater than the object to disrupt an object's inertia. A soccer ball will sit immobile on the playing field until a well-aimed kick sets it into motion.

God's people had experienced generations of spiritual inertia when Hezekiah became king seven centuries before Christ's birth. The Bible tells us Hezekiah was a godly man: "He did what the Lord considered right, as his ancestor David had done" (2 Chronicles 29:2). Hezekiah is remembered for his willingness to interrupt generations of apathy and compromise and for returning Israel to single-minded worship of God. He focused on repairing the nation's place of worship and on encouraging his people to recommit themselves to God.

After generations of neglect, it took a surprisingly short amount of time for the people to accomplish these tasks. Hezekiah's decision halted his people's inertia. When all was in readiness, Hezekiah invited his leaders to join him in worship at the dawn of a new day. Renewal came to the nation.

Is there an area of your life that has suffered from spiritual neglect? Today you can commit to return to God in this area.

Just Ask

If any of you needs wisdom to know what you should do, you should ask God, and he will give it to you. God is generous to everyone and doesn't find fault with them. When you ask for something, don't have any doubts.

James 1:5–6

Who do you turn to for advice? A friend or family member? Your pastor? Or do you turn to the advice offered by celebrities, magazines, and the internet? Some searches for advice depend on the level of desperation or the level of resources available. If you're desperate, you might turn to the first available source you can find or to those you can afford. But sometimes these sources of wisdom aren't very wise at all.

Perhaps you're searching for answers right now but aren't sure where to turn for wise guidance—especially in the middle of the night. If so, James the brother of Jesus has some advice for you: turn to God tonight for the wisdom and the knowledge you seek. Generously, He gives answers to those who seek His counsel. His answers and awesome solutions come from His Word or through the wise counsel of others who seek Him. Best of all, you don't have to pay a fortune to attain it.

Tonight, ask God for a supply of His never-ending wisdom. As you drift off in the still of the night, answers will assuredly come.

No Matter What

When he tests me, I'll come out as pure as gold. I have followed his footsteps closely. I have stayed on his path and did not turn from it. I have not left his commands behind. I have treasured his words in my heart.

Job 23:10–12

Picture this: You're running late and can't find your glasses. You dig through your purse, the pocket of the coat you wore yesterday, and between the couch cushions. When they don't materialize, you rush through the house frantically looking everywhere for your missing specs. Fifteen frustrating minutes pass, and you reach for your cell phone to let the person you're meeting know that you're running late. And there they are . . . sitting right where you had put them so you wouldn't forget where they were.

Most of us are prone to the temptation to run here and there looking for a solution when we're in the midst of a challenging situation. Job had experienced one extremely intense test after another, and his wife and friends encouraged him to do something to put an end to the fiery trials (as if he could). Job refused, knowing that the "solutions" suggested to him by others would send him running in a dozen wrong directions. So, he would stay the course and trust God no matter what happened.

Are you going through a trial right now? Have well-meaning friends and family members suggested solutions to you that would send you running in a direction God has not called you to go? In the stillness of these moments with the Lord before you launch into your day, affirm your willingness to stay on His path, and walk according to His Word no matter what happens.

In the Midst of the Storm

Remember the LORD of Armies is holy. He is the One you should fear and the one you should be terrified of.

Isaiah 8:13

The fear of the unknown is often worse than the imagined event. It can keep you awake at night fretting about the right decision or outcome. It can also make you feel as if you're about to face a horrible storm without any protection or provisions.

Knowing of His people's tendency to fear the unknown, God spoke a warning to the prophet Isaiah. God's prophet was not to fear the anger or disapproval of the people as he preached God's promise of the destruction of the northern kingdom of Israel and the Arameans at the hands of the Assyrians. While the people of Judah might delight at the destruction of their enemies, Isaiah could not rejoice, for he knew that the event was an act of judgment on God's part because of His people's great disobedience. God reminded Isaiah and the people of Judah that the Lord was the only One they were to fear.

Tonight, perhaps you feel as if the storm is upon you. Whether it is your marriage, your relationship with others, or ethical decisions to be made at work, remember Isaiah's words. The Lord of the Armies is the One to fear. But this kind of fear is healthy fear; it's the kind of fear that understands God's great power and rests in awe of it. Remember, He is with you. In the midst of the storm, His sun will shine for you.

Your Protector

Let all godly people pray to you when you may be found. Then raging floodwater will not reach them. You are my hiding place. You protect me from trouble. You surround me with joyous songs of salvation.

Psalm 32:6–7

A small child stumbles and falls down on the front porch. She picks herself up and runs to Mama weeping. Mama scoops up the youngster, examines the injury and holds her close. What a picture of comfort. You can just imagine how the child feels: safe and protected.

When difficulties arise and raging floodwaters flow around you, where do you go to find peace and comfort? David, the writer of Psalm 32, suggests a place of refuge—one that he sought many times in his life. This place of refuge is easily accessed by prayer.

When trouble comes your way, whether it is a small puddle or a monsoon of violent downpour, God can protect you. He will listen to your sorrows and hold you close in His big, strong arms. His love can give you strength to step out into the world again, braver and stronger than before. His songs will lift your soul from doubt and confusion. The Lord can even instruct you, just like a mother instructs her child. He can teach you what to do and where you should go. His eyes never lose sight of you.

So like the small child, run to your protector. Run to Jesus when you fall. He will scoop you up and hold you close.

Large and in Charge

"You put everything under his control." When God put every-thing under his Son's control, nothing was left out.

Hebrews 2:8

What would a typical day be like if everything seemed totally in control? Would your kids be perfectly behaved with no screaming fits, no lost homework, no complaints about food, no arguments about whose turn it is to do the dishes? Would they go to bed exactly when they're told without an argument? Would your co-workers and supervisor praise you and cooperate? Seems like a fantasy. After all, life is messy, life is hard, and it very often feels like we've lost control. We feel like a person in a runaway hot-air balloon, struggling with the ballast to maintain control.

Perhaps you've had an out-of-control day that has left you feeling exhausted tonight. How great it is, though, that we have a God who doesn't lose control. In fact, the writer of Hebrews specially mentions that "nothing was left out" of God's control. Even all the tiny details of our day that we so often forget, He has under His control.

Tonight, rest easy in the arms of the God who has absolutely everything under control. Trust Him to provide for you as He has promised. No matter how much comes your way, it will never be too much, because your heavenly Father is in charge, and He knows what He's doing. He's the only one who is really large and in charge.

A Mighty Fortress

God is our refuge and strength, an ever-present help in times of trouble. . . . The LORD of Armies is with us. The God of Jacob is our stronghold.

Psalm 46:1, 7

The newspapers and televised news stories show pictures of war-torn areas. But sometimes a home or an office building can be a place of war, thanks to misunderstandings and grievances. Various types of battles await each of us daily. Interpersonal conflicts (such as troubles with a co-worker or spouse) make everyday life a war zone because relationships test our faith. In reality, our enemies are not physical, but spiritual (see, for example, Ephesians 6:10–12). The battle is for our hearts.

Fights with family members or co-workers make us want to retreat into a safe environment. But if home itself is a war zone, we might try to protect ourselves from pain by erecting barriers around our hearts. We know these to be defense mechanisms which take the form of sarcasm, humor (laughing to ignore the pain), silence, and other behaviors. But God's refuge is stronger than any walls we might build up around our hearts. As the psalmist suggests, God's strength provides a formidable barrier against the worries of this world. Only He can provide a fortress for our hearts.

Today, you can face the battles of life knowing you are safe in God's fortress and that you fight with His loaned strength. When things get overwhelming this morning, close your eyes and envision His fortress of love surrounding you. You are not fighting this battle alone.

Well-Tended

I, the LORD, watch over it. I water it continually. I watch over it day and night so that no one will harm it.

Isaiah 27:3

To be watched over, fed, and protected by the Most High, the all-powerful God—what a picture of tenderness and strength, affection, and care. It is akin to a huge NFL football star rushing home every night to check on his African violets, hurrying down to the kitchen every morning to check for any new blooms, to trim off any old, and to carefully check the soil for moisture and health.

The prophet Isaiah preached a message of the future deliverance of Israel. In it he described God's people as a vineyard carefully nurtured by God. A good vineyard owner kept his or her vineyard watered and protected. Watering a vineyard "continually" in the arid climate of Palestine took a tremendous amount of effort. So the image Isaiah provides shows the efforts God promised to make on behalf of His people. His nurturing would cause His people to thrive.

As God's people—the church—we can take this message to heart as well. Often, we're so caught up in helping others to thrive that we neglect our own growth. But God promises to carefully watch over His little tender "plants." He waters you through His Word and protects you.

Let the wonder of God's concern sink in tonight as you get ready for bed. Know that even as you sleep, your heavenly Father is here, guiding your path and protecting you. His unfailing love for you is evident today, tonight, and tomorrow.

The Immensity of the Father

*The LORD, the only true God, has spoken. He has summoned
the earth from where the sun rises to where it sets.*

Psalm 50:1

How magnificent is your God! This morning, dwell upon His vast
power and the capability of His benevolent hands. As the psalmist
proclaims, only the Lord could claim the earth as a witness of
His trustworthiness to keep a covenant. If He seems too vast for
comprehension, study His many names and be encouraged. He is
God Almighty (Genesis 17:1), Wonderful Counselor and Prince of
Peace (Isaiah 9:6), Abba (Mark 14:36), Father (Luke 11:2). The
names of your Father allow you to see the facets of His character.
As you study His names, watch His greatness spread out before
you each day, even as you come to know Him more intimately.

The character of your heavenly Father is like that of the
ocean—vast, awe-inspiring, powerful. Every day the sea is renewed before your eyes and the longer you watch, the better you
come to know it. It is pearly and calm on a mild spring dawn,
brilliantly blue under the summer sun, wild and foaming in a
winter storm, and glowing silver beneath a rising moon. You
cannot know the character of the Father at a glance, but you can
know Him more each day simply by being with Him. Trust Him
to reveal Himself to you.

Your great Father cares for you, His precious daughter. He
who has "summoned the earth" is strong enough to carry any
burden. Trust Him and "turn all your anxiety over to God because
he cares for you" (1 Peter 5:7).

At the Crossroads

This is what the LORD says: Stand at the crossroads and look. Ask which paths are the old, reliable paths. Ask which way leads to blessings. Live that way, and find a resting place for yourselves.

Jeremiah 6:16

Standing at the crossroads—what image does that bring to mind? Detective movies where the skilled sleuth confronts two possible roads on which the kidnapper's car traveled? Robert Frost's poem, "The Road Not Taken," which begins, "Two roads diverged in a yellow wood"? Or, perhaps you think of an unmarked, country intersection when you've taken a detour or shortcut and are trying to find your way back to the main highway.

In trying to convince a wayward people to return to Him, God spoke the message above through the prophet Jeremiah. He reminded them to consider how their ancestors worshiped God. This was the road to follow. The other road, the road of rebellion that led to their present predicament (threatened with invasion), had led them astray. So, they had a choice to make.

We're often faced with difficult choices. Knowing that these choices are not always straightforward, our heavenly Father has given us some guidelines in making these tough, life-changing decisions. We can find these "tried and true" paths in the Bible and through the wise counsel of others.

Tonight, pray for guidance and for clarity with the big decisions facing you and those you love. Pray that He will show you the right path to take and for the courage to walk that path.

Sing a Song

But I will sing about your strength. In the morning I will joy-fully sing about your mercy. You have been my stronghold and a place of safety in times of trouble.

Psalm 59:16

A few decades ago, a Christian couple from Hawaii decided to begin a music ministry. They hit the recording studio and then hit the road, traveling to churches and concert halls across the nation. Aptly named "The Hawaiians," they presented island music with a gospel message. When introducing his wife to the audience, the husband would speak of her amazing ability to sing a clear and strong high C immediately upon waking in the morning.

The thought of singing a high C first thing in the morning might seem laughable to you. You may, in fact, not even know what a high C sounds like! And this might be one of those days when the weight of all your cares is so heavy, well, who would even want to sing?

As God's daughter, you can go to your Father with songs of joy or sorrow. Sing, "Abba," which simply means, "Daddy." The pure music from the heart of a woman of God, whether in jubilation or grief, will be welcomed by Him. As David the psalmist and a skilled musician in his own right suggested, God will meet your needs with strength and mercy. He will be your stronghold and place of safety during the rough patches.

No matter what your voice sounds like in this world, know that your song is more precious to God's ears than the voices of angels. Sing a song of praise to Him right now.

The Real Eternal Flame

He was the source of life, and that life was the light for humanity. The light shines in the dark, and the dark has never extinguished it.

John 1:4–5

All over the world, eternal flames—torches that burn continually—are lit to commemorate the lives of those lost in war or to some other tragedy. This symbol of never-ending fire transcends cultures and even generations as it honors life and recognizes loss. But these flames, however well-intended and well-constructed, go out. A strong wind or rain comes along, the government regime changes, or the supply of oil doesn't get replenished, and the flame is gone.

Even the Olympic flame—carried by a series of runners over many months to ignite the torch wherever the games are held—eventually goes out.

How different, then, is the light that Jesus brought into the world, as the apostle John explains. The darkness has never and will never extinguish this light! We can have hope, because our Savior, the source of life, has come to us and lived among us.

And it keeps getting better. Through the Holy Spirit, this flame now lives inside each of us. Even when life seems hard and dark, even when that light seems dim and distant, we can trust that what God has promised is true. He has promised to guide us, to be with us, and to light our way. Tonight, as you turn off your bedside light, remember the light that burns inside of you: Jesus in you.

Life's Deserts

O God, you are my God. At dawn I search for you. My soul thirsts for you. My body longs for you in a dry, parched land where there is no water.

Psalm 63:1

Have you ever found yourself feeling that you are in a "dry, parched land where there is no water"? Does it seem like the spark of life has disappeared even from your relationship with God? It's hot and exhausting to be in the desert of the soul—dried up spiritually.

David had done his share of running and hiding in the desert as he was hunted by King Saul. But when David found himself feeling dry and weary, he sought after his heavenly Father and declared, "My soul clings to you. Your right hand supports me" (63:8). David did not wait until he felt fulfilled—he actively sought after and clung to God!

Throughout the Psalms, David's laments are full of sorrow. God felt so far away. Perhaps you know how it feels to search for God as dawn breaks. You have felt the days stretch before you like a desert. It might be a rocky desert, full of specific trials that assail you, or it might be a desert of endless dunes that exhausts you. Either way, you long for the relief of an oasis; you long for comfort from your heavenly Father.

When you are in a desert and God seems far away, follow David's example. Cling to God and say to Him, "You have been my help. In the shadow of your wings, I sing joyfully" (63:7).

The Ultimate Guardian

God can guard you so that you don't fall and so that you can be full of joy as you stand in his glorious presence without fault.

Jude 24

Lifeguards, security guards, border guards, guard dogs, the coast guard, crossing guards, computer safeguards, CheckGuard—there are many types of guards in our society to make sure we're doing the right thing and to prevent us from getting into trouble. Some of these guards, particularly the computer safeguards, can seem troublesome with their constant demands for safety checks and upgrades. Nevertheless, we know they are there to keep our files secure from viruses and other hazards.

Just as we have this earthly protection, the Bible promises that God also guards us. He protects us not only from the physical dangers we encounter but also guards our joy. He can keep us from being tempted to do those things we shouldn't so that in heaven we can celebrate His presence without shame. Unlike the earthly guards that go off duty sometimes, God is never off duty.

What might prevent you from asking for His protection tonight? A sense of self-sufficiency, perhaps, or a guilty pleasure that you know you shouldn't continue? Or perhaps you wonder if God really will do for you what Jude the brother of Jesus described.

Jesus calls to you to trust that He will do what He promised: to guard you until you reach His "glorious presence." Are you willing?

Sun Sparkles

May they fear you as long as the sun and moon shine—throughout every generation.

Psalm 72:5

Sometimes the sky is so bright and clear, the sun so warm and intense, that we almost feel we could reach out and touch its very rays, grabbing them to save in our pocket for a rainy day. Sunbeams have a magical quality. They bring warmth and smiles to the faces of people across all generations—from the youngest child set free to run in the field to the oldest woman sitting in her front porch swing. God's creation truly has a magical quality, and along with the psalmist, we long for people throughout every generation to know God and be in awe of Him.

You have the opportunity to shape the future by teaching the next generation about God. As wise King Solomon suggested in Psalm 72, the fear or reverence of the Lord is a goal to strive for. God draws us to Himself through His truth. The love He has shown you through His Son Jesus Christ will last far longer than your lifetime. Just as the sun will thrive long after your last breath, the gospel will ring true into eternity.

As you begin this day, think about who you could impact today. Is there someone in your life who doesn't know about Jesus? Is there a younger person who needs encouragement? Make today a day of intentional legacy building. Celebrate the sunbeams with someone you love!

Starlit

You will be God's children without any faults among people who are crooked and corrupt. You will shine like stars among them in the world as you hold firmly to the word of life.

Philippians 2:15–16

What must the night sky have looked like two thousand years ago, before incandescent bulbs, jets flying overhead, searchlights advertising the new mall that just opened up across town, street-lights, industrial pollution, high rises, and radio towers with their airplane-warning antennae blinking on top?

It must have been brilliant and mysterious. The sun sets, and the first stars appear in the twilight, out of "nowhere," peppering the sky, until the black is awash with pinpoints of light twinkling as far as the eye can see.

This is the picture the Philippians had in mind as Paul called them to live differently from those around them. He called them, and he calls us, to consciously move away from the normal patterns of this world—and to live in such a way that we "shine." This is not easy. We want to complain when we're forced to wait for an hour at the dentist's office. Don't they know how precious our time is? We want to argue when our neighbor complains that our lawn is not up to his or her standards. But we are called to be different so that through us the light of our Father in heaven can touch the heart of our neighbor, or maybe the receptionist at the dentist's office, so that she might also find the love that we have found in Jesus Christ our Lord.

Tonight, commit to shining like a star—living in such a way that God is honored.

A Fresh Start

*Satisfy us every morning with your mercy so that we may sing
joyfully and rejoice all our days.*

Psalm 90:14

Each new day brings the chance to start your life off fresh. The
sun's rays stretch out their beams of light across the horizon,
reaching higher and higher across the backdrop of the endless
blue-hued atmosphere, reminding you that you too can stretch out
across your world and make an impact. Your dreams and goals
expand with each faith-filled thought, and your possibilities are
ever growing as you seek the Lord's guidance.

Sometimes your dreams may be simple. Sometimes your goal
may simply be to make it through the day with a smile on your
face, even if your forecast turns to showers. The magnitude of
the thought isn't the focus; your dependence on God is what
matters. Today, you have a brand-new chance to live your life
closer to the Lord.

What dreams are in your heart today? What thoughts fill
your mind with joy? Dare to dream of a life more abundant than
yesterday—a life full of joy and praise to the Father.

Dear friend, the Lord loves you. He sings over you and rejoices that you are His child. Doesn't that bring a sweet melody
of gratitude to your lips? Sing to Him today. As you start your
day, sing a song of praise to God.

Tipping the Scales

A person's anxiety will weigh him down, but an encouraging word makes him joyful.

Proverbs 12:25

It starts gradually—something unexpected arises, there's a change of plans, the weather doesn't cooperate, and what started out to be a good day suddenly turns into stress. Anxiety tips the scales of your life as you feel a headache coming on, the blood pressure rising, and everything turning into a big deal. You start wondering how you're ever going to make it through the day.

And then a friend calls just to say hi and that she's thinking of you. You talk for a couple of minutes, and suddenly the scale tips once again as the world rights itself, and you remember to breathe again.

Our heavenly Father knew we needed that. He put us here, not to live alone, but to support each other. He gives us friends, brothers and sisters, and sometimes complete strangers, to remind us of those basic promises: "You're special." "You're beautiful." "You're doing a good job; keep up the hard work." "You know what, you're fantastic!" or even "Don't worry; God can handle it" when you're faced with those days that might seem overwhelming. God sends His messengers to help you remember His promises.

Tonight, thank God for the people He has given you to encourage you. Ask Him to show you who might need that same encouraging word tomorrow.

Out of Sight

As high as the heavens are above the earth—that is how vast his mercy is toward those who fear him. As far as the east is from the west—that is how far he has removed our rebellious acts from himself.

Psalm 103:11–12

Think about the marvelous promises within these verses: the mercy God provides is boundless, and He will be faithful to remove your sins from you by an immeasurable distance.

Why is God willing to do such a thing for you? Maybe we need to go back to the Garden of Eden to find out.

God never intended that His creation should suffer. But when Eve gave in to temptation, suffering became a part of His perfect universe. One small act of disobedience resulted in all of humanity needing a Savior who could reconcile them with God. Because of His great mercy, Jesus became the Savior through His sacrifice on the cross, followed by His glorious resurrection.

So what's your part in the equation? If you are born again, then Jesus Christ is your Savior. Therefore, when you commit rebellious acts (sins) and genuinely repent, Jesus removes your sins from you, and from Himself, as far as the east is from the west.

Hard to understand, isn't it? The Creator loves you—and every person—so much He provided a way for you to be blameless, spotless, and pure. No matter how you've disappointed God by what you've thought, done, or left undone, by your act of repentance coupled with His vast mercy, it's all gone!

Gone. Out of sight. Out of mind.

That's something to smile about all day long.

Eagerly Looking

With my soul I long for you at night. Yes, with my spirit I eagerly look for you. When your guiding principles are on earth, those who live in the world learn to do what is right.

Isaiah 26:9

During the day we're on task and productive. When the stillness of the night closes in, however, we're left with time to ponder over things we've done or said in the midst of our demanding life—things that escaped us in our busyness, but stand out boldly in the solitude of evening. "Why was I so short with my mom?" "I really overreacted to that comment at work." "How could I have forgotten to ask Sue about her doctor appointment?" It is then that we realize how much or how little we've involved the Lord in our day. It is then that our souls focus on God. In those quiet moments, we long to be closer, more attentive. We want to learn His principles so that we do more right than wrong in the course of our days. With Isaiah we cry out, "I long for you at night. Yes, with my spirit I eagerly look for you."

God's Word gives clarity and wisdom to apply to daily living. As you make your search for the Lord (and all He is) a part of your nightly ritual, as you eagerly look for Him, you will see that He is waiting for you. The more evening moments you spend eagerly looking for Him, the more your character will resemble His in the mornings.

So in these quiet moments, trust that as you eagerly search for God, He is waiting for you. He promises guidance, wisdom, and yes, forgiveness. He will give you blessed rest so that tomorrow you will be ready to walk into the new day with Him.

Good Food

Let them give thanks to the LORD because of his mercy. He performed his miracles for Adam's descendants. He gave plenty to drink to those who were thirsty. He filled those who were hungry with good food.

Psalm 107:8–9

If you've ever been on a diet or are a health-conscious woman, you know what constitutes good food: fresh fruits and vegetables, lean meats, low carbs, and as little fat as possible. Candy bars, potato chips, and chocolate (unfortunately!) are considered the enemy.

The Bible mentions food and drink quite often, from the miraculous manna which fell from heaven and fed the Hebrews in the wilderness to Jesus feeding over five thousand people with only a few loaves of bread and some fish.

Yet the most important reference to food is when Jesus proclaims that He is the bread of life (John 6:35) and giver of living water (John 4:10). You might think it strange that Jesus uses such common fare to describe Himself. Yet what is more important to sustain life than bread and water?

You can partake of this amazing sustenance. How? By opening your Bible. Feast upon God's Word. Drink in the message He has for you each day. The psalm writer exclaims that God will give plenty to drink to those who are thirsty and fill the hungry with good food. Feasting in this way will help you develop excellent spiritual health. And the more you devour, the hungrier you'll be for more.

Start each morning with a balanced breakfast, including a healthy helping of God's Word. After all, it's the most important meal of the day!

Open 24/7

Your gates will always be open. They will never be closed day or night so that people may bring you the wealth of nations.

Isaiah 60:11

If you have to fill a prescription in the middle of the night, you know the value of an all-night pharmacy. Or, if you discover at midnight that you need milk for the morning, you understand the worth of a grocery store that is always open. And then there's the diner on the corner that's open in the wee hours of the morning when you're up and out early and need that first cup of coffee.

The image described in this verse from the book of Isaiah relates to a Jerusalem restored by the glory of the Lord. No longer would the city be locked up tight against invading armies. Instead, it would be open to all. Nations would bring wealth, instead of taking the wealth of Jerusalem's citizens.

What does your spirit need tonight? Whether you are longing for comfort, wisdom, courage, or a simple confirmation that you're loved, you will not be denied. The Lord is always open for business.

As you close your eyes, picture that "open" sign at your favorite all-night drugstore or coffee shop—that inviting neon that lets you know they're open for business. Then remember that access to God is also always "open." Walk through and know that He is always there for you whenever you need Him, even in the middle of the night.

Share the Music

My heart is confident, O God. I want to sing and make music even with my soul. Wake up, harp and lyre! I want to wake up at dawn.

Psalm 108:1–2

A popular Christian musician once stated in an interview that he would often wake up with the sunrise as that was the best time to write music. He said there were times when he'd fall asleep with music in his soul and awaken with song lyrics in his mind.

This musician isn't the only person who feels the Savior's music in his soul. Like a tune that turns over and over in your mind, the blessings of God should fill your heart to overflowing. And when the love spills over, there's nothing else to do but share it with those around you.

As a Christian, you are called by God to share His love. Take a moment and think about how you, personally, have done just that. Remember that any simple act of kindness toward others allows God's love to shine through you. You held the door at the mall for the lady with the massive stroller. You smiled and spoke kindly to the waitress who was obviously having a bad day. You didn't lose your temper when a co-worker misplaced important paperwork. You helped your child with his homework.

You might say, "Oh, come on. Doing those things comes naturally!"

Not to everyone. Because you are filled with the love of Jesus, His light shines through you. Be ready for the time when someone asks, "What is it that makes you different?" Trust that He will make your heart confident as you share the music.

A Bit of Solitude

After sending the people away, he went up a mountain to pray by himself. When evening came, he was there alone.

Matthew 14:23

When bedtime finally comes and the only sound is the night settling in, what do you do first? Do you grab the remote off your nightstand and flip to a rerun of your favorite old sitcom? Do you search for the ads in the newspaper to see who's having the best sales on new shoes? Or do you take this time to be alone with God?

Jesus knew what it was like to be surrounded by people demanding His attention all day. What they asked of Him was all-consuming and He was the only one who could deliver. For those reasons, He made it a priority to slip away from everyone in the dark of night to spend time with His Father.

Do you have times of solitude where you can talk freely to your Father? As day becomes night and the day's work is over, find a place where you can hear from the Lord a little easier than through the din of the busy day. You may find that solitude in the middle of your bed, snuggled up in your robe on the sofa, or soaking in a warm tub. The important thing is to find a private place to meet your Lord and pray.

Splendor on the Journey

But the path of righteous people is like the light of dawn that becomes brighter and brighter until it reaches midday.

Proverbs 4:18

From a faint glimpse on the horizon to the brilliance of the noon-day sun, the rising path of colors and heat shift and shape the sun as it inches above the earth's edge. What begins as the tiniest display becomes a bold proclamation of heat, rays, and light.

Do you remember the day you first heard about God? Your initial brush with the divine has merged with the many days of faith-building since, creating a faint light, then a stronger light in the world. You are a witness to those around you, showing others what it means to be a Christian. Think about how much you've already grown in faith since you began your Christian journey. Just as you've come this far, you also have a long adventure ahead—a beautiful and glorious journey with the Lord. The sun rises, peaks at noonday, but has a longer path ahead as it travels toward sunset.

Today, celebrate who you are in Christ. Don't forget, Jesus says you are the light of the world. Take time to dwell on the layers of your faith and how each opportunity for growth is like the colorful layers of the sun's rising and setting. The many layers of who God has created you to be become a beautiful display for the world around you to see. Others will see who you are, what you believe, and how God is using you for His glory.

Deal of a Lifetime

My son, obey the command of your father, and do not disregard the teachings of your mother. . . . Hang them around your neck. When you walk around, they will lead you. When you lie down, they will watch over you.

Proverbs 6:20–22

Remember going to bed when you were little? Some of us had bedtime rituals as children that included being tucked in and praying with a parent. When such a ritual becomes ingrained within us, we can't help passing it on to our children.

These verses in Proverbs encourage the passing on of knowledge. While they can be taken literally, the verses are meant to show the importance of learning to apply wisdom permanently to our lives. Imagine putting on the most beautiful necklace you can ever imagine. Putting on wisdom is like wearing a priceless piece of jewelry. Wisdom will add depth, honor, and the ability to live more confidently. When we walk in the wisdom the Lord provides, He will keep us on the right path and remove all obstacles.

The last line is especially comforting. It refers to one of the covenant blessings from Leviticus 26:6: "I will bring peace to your land. You will lie down with no one to scare you."

When we follow God, we enter into a special deal with Him. He has laid out some specific guidelines to follow and promises that when we do, He'll bless us in special ways for our obedience. No deal you'll ever be offered or contract you'll ever sign will be this easy, direct, or as completely fulfilled. It's very simple: seek and apply His teachings to your life and He will fill your sleepless nights with peace. Are you in?

Genuine Gold

Your faith is more precious than gold, and by passing the test, it gives praise, glory, and honor to God.

1 Peter 1:7

Since prehistoric times, gold has been known and valued for its splendor and strength. It's mentioned frequently in the Old Testament, starting with Genesis 2:11, and is one of the gifts from the wise men to Jesus. In medieval times, gold was often seen as beneficial for health, reasoning that something that scarce and beautiful had to be healthy. Today, the top prize from the Nobel Prizes to the Olympics are gold medals. Scripture tells us that in heaven the streets are paved with gold (Revelation 21:21).

Gold's yellow color and reflective property make it quite eye-catching. Pure gold withstands heat and is eternal—it does not tarnish or corrode.

Perhaps these qualities are why faith is compared to gold. Your loving heavenly Father wants you to have a pure, strong, and healthy faith in Him. Life's trials and troubles can mature your faith if you let them. And when you have genuine faith, then you are reflective of God.

This morning, remember that your suffering, disappointment, frustration, questioning, or doubt is temporary and, as it passes through this fire of testing, will only become stronger.

Now put on some glittery gold jewelry (even if it isn't real!) and smile that your faith is genuine gold.

Waiting on Him

My soul waits for the LORD more than those who watch for the morning, more than those who watch for the morning.

Psalm 130:6

Some nights the ticking of the bedside clock sounds like a beating drum. We long for the Lord to make His presence known and bring with Him peaceful music to quiet the sounds of wakefulness. We glance frequently toward the window hoping His comforting spirit will win the race and beat the gray light of morning. We toss and turn, never comfortable, and even when we close our eyes we don't drift off.

The writer of Psalm 130 eloquently expressed what it means to wait in wakefulness on the Lord. Wakefulness and waiting indicate an unmet need or expectation. What are you waiting for? For the pain to subside? For God's intervention in a stressful situation? Waiting on the Lord isn't an empty exercise but an act of worship. Waiting means expecting Him to answer.

As you wait, lay your head gently on the pillow. Know that the Holy Spirit is already with you and offers more comfort than you could imagine. He is peace and promises to meet your needs. Let His presence lull you to sleep knowing that He is able to handle all your worries and problems.

A Heart Mirror

As a face is reflected in water, so a person is reflected by his heart.
Proverbs 27:19

Toddlers love to look at themselves in mirrors. They giggle and laugh, making faces at their image. Watch them get closer, turn sideways and raise their eyes wide open. They scrutinize their reactions. They probably even give a sloppy kiss to the new friend in the glass—who kisses them right back! What amazing detail their faces portray! What sweet, unblemished joy!

As you get older, mirrors become more of a necessity than a joy. You want to make sure your hair isn't sticking in all directions and that your lipstick is only stuck to your lips and not your teeth. You want to look your best, and the mirror helps you see yourself clearly.

Yet that's only a part of who you are. A mirror doesn't show what you're really like deep on the inside. That, as the verse says, is reflected by your heart.

You probably spend a good amount of time in front of the mirror, but how much time do you spend examining the details of your inner life? What does your heart say about you? Just like a mirror reflects a person's face, so your actions portray your heart. It's good to occasionally sit quietly and examine your expression to the world. What do other people see when they're with you?

Jesus can help you improve your reflection. Simply ask Him for assistance. Ask that His glory will shine through you in all you do.

Weeping, Then Joy

His anger lasts only a moment. His favor lasts a lifetime. Weeping may last for the night, but there is a song of joy in the morning.

Psalm 30:5

Our emotions often rise closer to the surface at night. We successfully bury feelings of loneliness, sadness, fear, longing, or shame as we move at double-time during the day, but at bedtime they can rise up. We sometimes put our minds through endless loops of memory tapes—of regrets from our past or "what-ifs" from the future as we lie awake in the dark. On occasion, the swell of it is too big and must be released. Then we weep.

God created us as emotional beings. David, the king of Israel, was considered to be a man after God's own heart (1 Samuel 13:14; 16:12). As one who wholeheartedly worshiped the Lord, he didn't hold back when it came to expressing his feelings. Some of the most emotionally vivid psalms in the Bible were penned by David. No stranger to nights of weeping, David provides a message of hope even in the midst of a time of weeping.

Being overtaken by your out-of-control emotions is only for a little while. Don't deny yourself the right to cry, but let your tears fall in the lap of One who cares most: Jesus.

Remember the times God took you through an emotion-filled night, never leaving you to weep alone. He loves you. You are one of His favorites. This is true for all time. And, while you may be burdened tonight, He promises to fill your heart with a different emotion tomorrow: joy.

Diving into Your Day

The day and the night are yours. You set the moon and the sun in their places.

Psalm 74:16

Some days you awaken, sit on the edge of your bed, and wonder what you'll be diving into today. Maybe it's a pool of busyness, or of concern, or of leftover trouble from yesterday. Looking down, you're not sure you're ready to take the dive. After all, it could end up being cool and refreshing—the situation could turn out positive. Or it could end up being a difficult dive with a rather painful "belly flop" to finish it off.

The psalmist proclaims the truth that God owns today, your day, and that His power set the moon and sun in their places. The writer trusted that God would deliver him from his enemies. He cried out to the Lord, asking God to remember him and his people as they were surrounded by trouble. He didn't know what he'd be diving into, but he wanted God there to catch him.

What are you diving into today? Take your stance and don't look down; instead, look up to God. Stand in the bold truth that the Lord has created your day and night, and He will also take care of you in your today and tomorrow. Though you may feel unsure of what the day will bring, God is leading you. He is mighty enough to create the planets and life from nothing, and He is powerful enough to carry you through this situation.

Remember Him Tonight

As I lie on my bed, I remember you. Through the long hours of the night, I think about you.

Psalm 63:6

Lying down at night, supported by the familiar comfort of your own bed, do you sometimes find that while your body is tired, your mind is wide awake? What occupies your thoughts? Are your emotions or worries robbing you of sound sleep? Sometimes our emotions, like the rapids of a river, continually carry us away even as we struggle back toward the shores of sleep.

David the psalmist-king probably had many sleepless nights too, but he redirected his emotion-filled soul to thoughts of God. All through Psalm 63, David describes attributes of God such as His power, His love, and His mercy. He considered the times when God came to his rescue. In short, David determined to praise rather than focus on his worries.

While you lie awake, you can take control of your thoughts just as David did and release the tight grip your emotions have on you. Let your mind focus on the One who holds all your concerns in His loving hands. Be assured that He is full of mercy, grace, and for you in your warm bed this minute.

Remember all that He did for David. What wouldn't He do for you? What couldn't He do? Not one of your concerns is too big or remotely impossible for the God of David, who is also your God. Ease into sleep with David's song of praise filling your soul.

Last Words

The one who rules humans with justice rules with the fear of God. He is like the morning light as the sun rises, like a morning without clouds, like the brightness after a rainstorm. The rain makes the grass grow from the earth.

2 Samuel 23:3–4

Whether it is a whispered "I love you" or an expression of fear or remorse, a dying person's last words are often weighted with profound meaning to those who are left behind. Last words may capture the essence of the way a person has lived, or they may open a window on what the person is experiencing as he or she is about to inhale eternity for the first time. In some cases, they do both.

This morning's Scripture passage is drawn from King David's final words. He used his last few breaths to reflect on his life's calling as a leader. David communicated the idea that the best, fairest leaders simply mirror the purity of the white-gold light of a sunrise over a cloudless horizon and the sparkling, life-giving growth seen in grass after a gentle rain.

David's last words were far more than leadership instructions, however. His words expressed a sense of childlike awe as David basked in the beauty and character of his Creator and readied to meet Him face-to-face.

What would your final words be this morning? It is a sobering question, to be sure. Would they be words of hope, as David's were, or of sadness, fear, or regret? Take a few moments this morning to prayerfully contemplate your answer—and purpose to live today in light of your prayer.

Unimaginable Peace

In every situation let God know what you need in prayers and requests while giving thanks. Then God's peace, which goes beyond anything we can imagine, will guard your thoughts and emotions through Christ Jesus.

Philippians 4:6–7

If you have ever spent the day gardening, you know this kind of work will give you stiff knees and an aching back. But gardening is also wonderfully rewarding. Any time spent connecting with the earth is life affirming. Best of all, when bedtime comes after a day of physical work, sleep feels absolutely delicious!

Prayer is a form of nighttime gardening. We till the soil by creating regular prayer times. Then we plant our worries in the enveloping soil of God's love. Expressing thanks for this opportunity for spiritual growth, we are blessed with an immediate harvest. A deep sense of peace settles over our bodies, allowing us to drift gently into sleep.

This passage is almost a how-to manual for our nighttime garden. The apostle Paul tells us to begin by expressing our needs and requests in the form of prayers. We add to each prayer an expression of gratitude. Before God answers us, we offer thanks. By doing this we are saying, "I trust in You, Lord. I know You are listening and will help me." Through these simple acts of faith, we are freed from worry. Our burdens are planted in the dark of night. Peace is the harvest of a prayer garden.

Tonight is a great time to begin planting prayer and reaping peace! Ask Jesus to watch over the seeds you have planted. Then when you lie back on your pillow, sleep comes quickly.

He Owns Everything

The LORD wants you to obey his commands and laws that I'm giving you today for your own good. Remember that the sky, the highest heaven, the earth and everything it contains belong to the LORD your God.

Deuteronomy 10:13–14

Imagine you're outdoors. Look up at the infinite cobalt sky above your head. Maybe you see cotton ball clouds slowly float across the great expanse. Pretend you're scanning the landscape. Can you picture a lush, green hillside with speckled, plump cattle leisurely grazing? In the distance, you hear the lowing call from a lone calf searching for its mother.

Now, can you envision a gentle rain? Watch the tiny, iridescent droplets bounce off tree leaves and find their way down to the thirsty earth. As you visualize the glorious world our Lord created, may you be reminded that His greatest and most beloved creation is you. Since you're His most favored creation, He naturally wants only the best for you. His enormous mercy fashioned rules and boundaries so you could walk in His ways, love Him, and serve Him with all your heart and soul.

This verse in Deuteronomy urges obedience in response to a powerful and merciful God. The Israelites needed this reminder, too, as they set out on their journey.

This morning, as you sip on a steaming cup of fragrant tea or savor your mocha latte, remember that the heavens above, the earth beneath, and everything in between belongs to the great Creator—your heavenly Father. Rejoice today that He loves you more than everything else He made.

God Was Here

You are my hope, O Almighty Lord. You have been my confidence ever since I was young. I depended on you before I was born. You took me from my mother's womb. My songs of praise constantly speak about you.

Psalm 71:5–6

Imagine for a moment the psalmist David flipping through the mental photo album of his life as he writes this psalm. He's not young anymore—perhaps he's an old man as he flips through the events of his life. "There are my father and mother and brothers before I was born. . . . There's me as a baby. . . . That's when I was watching the sheep and playing my harp—those were good days. . . . Oh, and my friend Jonathan—what a good friend he was. . . . There's me when I first was crowned king. . . ." He recognizes that in every phase of his life, even the hard times, the words "God was here" were written on each event.

In your life, it is no different. God has been just as present in every stage—even before you knew Him, even when you couldn't sense His presence. As you prepare for bed tonight, flip back through your own photo album of memories. Think about how God has been present and faithful in each of those snapshots. You, too, could take a sticky note and plaster the words "God was here" on the photo album pages of your life. Every step of the way, right from the start, He has been by your side and will continue to be in the future.

In God's Garden

Can any of you add an hour to your life by worrying? If you can't do a small thing like that, why worry about other things? Consider how the flowers grow. They never work or spin yarn for clothes. But I say that not even Solomon in all his majesty was dressed like one of these flowers.

Luke 12:25–27

When spring arrives, many people pull out the gardening gloves and wheelbarrow and begin cleaning the garden of fall and winter leftovers. If you live in a climate that has cold winters, you know the joy of the warm breezes and the thrill of watching colorful crocuses peek up through the last coating of snow. The joy of planting a colorful bed of flowers that will last all summer keeps one motivated to pull weeds and dig dirt. Drop in a seed, add a little sunshine and water, and the beauty grows. In your garden, you've helped in the process, but only God brings the plants to their full glory.

Consider the flowers—they bring such beauty by just being. Perhaps you're carrying a load of worry, woe, or wishes this morning. That load strains your spirit and threatens to keep you from enjoying this day, ministering to others, or living carefree with the Father. Why not lay your spiritual load down before Him now? If He looks after the world's flower gardens, think how much He'll care for you. You're His prized blossom.

Forever

To the one who made the great lights—because his mercy endures forever. The sun to rule the day—because his mercy endures forever. The moon and stars to rule the night—because his mercy endures forever.

Psalm 136:7–9

What do you think of as you gaze at the moon and stars? While we might admire the beauty of a full moon and twinkling stars or take for granted that they are always present in the sky, the psalm writer used the moon and stars as signs of God's faithfulness and worthiness of worship. They are a testimony to the continuation of the seasons. The sun rises and sets, the moon waxes and wanes, the stars twinkle, and the years pass, all because of God's faithfulness.

Consider God's involvement in the seasons of your life. If you were to narrate your life or the events of your family as signs of His faithfulness, what events would you include? Perhaps your narration would go something like this: "To the One who healed my sister—because His mercy endures forever"; "To the One who gave my husband his job—because His mercy endures forever"; "To the One who gives us food to eat and a warm home to sleep in—because His mercy endures forever." Make this psalm your song—your chance to praise God for His presence and care for you. His mercy, His kindness, His faithfulness, and His love endure forever.

A Fork in the Road

Let me hear about your mercy in the morning, because I trust you. Let me know the way that I should go, because I long for you.

Psalm 143:8

It is easy to get lost in the countryside when you drive off the beaten path. What starts out as a simple trek down a straight road can become more difficult when you find there is a fork in the road. One subtle turn to the left or right and your path changes, while most of the time only one road leads to the desired destination. So, which road is the best one to take? You need to ask someone who knows the way.

God knows exactly what you need, how you feel, and how you make your decisions. Did you know that the Lord knows what you need before you ask Him? David, the king of Israel expressed his trust in God's counsel. God wants you to seek His counsel, even for the most insignificant choices in life. Isn't it incredible to think that God wants to be a part of your smallest decisions?

As you begin your morning, think about the details of your day and the areas of your life that need a fresh glimpse of God's presence. Imagine your options as a fork in the road, and ask the Lord to guide you in the way you should go. If you need God's mercy today, ask Him to lavish His love and mercy on you. Then watch for the ways He answers your prayer.

Planned Out

We know that all things work together for the good for those who love God—those whom he has called according to his plan.

Romans 8:28

Sometimes your day is so packed with activity that it's hard to think even five minutes ahead, let alone five days. But God knows what is ahead for you. Long ago, He planned out all of the days of your life: "Every day of my life was recorded in your book before one of them had taken place" (Psalm 139:16).

Knowing that your days are already prepared by God is a comforting thought. He has a plan for your life—one that is not random or confusing, but one full of purpose and meaning. God loves you and has the best for you, and this can give you hope even when it does not seem as though everything is working out for your good. The apostle Paul penned this powerful message—one that we don't always understand during the hard times. What you are unable to understand today is something that God will somehow use for your good and for His glory. Nothing is ever lost with God; all things will indeed work together for good.

God calls you His daughter, and His plan for your life is good and important. As you lie down tonight, meditate on God's kindness and on His Word—and trust that He is working everything out in your life for good.

Abundant Supply

The poor and needy are looking for water, but there is none. Their tongues are parched with thirst. I, the LORD . . . will make rivers flow on bare hilltops. I will make springs flow through valleys. I will turn deserts into lakes. I will turn dry land into springs.

Isaiah 41:17–18

Have you ever been so thirsty that your mouth felt like cotton? Maybe your tongue swelled and it was hard to speak or swallow. With each breath, your lips became more parched. While thirst can be a miserable sensation, God designed it to alert you to your body's daily requirement for water.

In the mountains of Idaho and other states, wildfires often rage on the dry, combustible ground. Firefighters risk their lives fighting the blistering, uncontrollable fires. Helicopters hover dangerously close to the dancing flames, dumping water in hopes of saturating the ground to extinguish the threat. A generous quantity of water is the salvation.

In a message of hope for the soon-to-be-exiled people of Israel, Isaiah used the metaphor of water to explain that God would provide for His people. No longer would they thirst for God's resources.

God also promises to provide for you. And the best part is He is not stingy. He pours out in abundance. You can live in constant supply of God's grace, wisdom, guidance, and love—if you ask. Out of His multiplied riches, He generously supplies all your needs.

Praise God for the bountiful things He has done and will do for you. Then, go get a tall, cool glass of water and take a long, satisfying drink.

Perfect Faithfulness

The Lord is faithful and will strengthen you and protect you against the evil one.

2 Thessalonians 3:3

What do you think of when you consider the word faithful? Geysers like Old Faithful? Friends or family members who are consistently "there" for you? *Encarta World English Dictionary* defines faithful as "consistently trustworthy and loyal, especially to a person, a promise, or duty." Yet even the most faithful of family members or friends sometimes falter in faithfulness, depending on their own life situations. Perhaps having experienced the disloyalty of others, you wonder if it is possible to ever find someone who is faithful.

The apostle Paul makes a strong case for the faithfulness of God. He encouraged his readers to rely on God to protect them against the harmful actions of "worthless and evil people" (3:2), actions inspired by the primary enemy of Christians—the "evil one" (Satan). In a time of persecution, a time when the believers in and around Thessalonica probably felt powerless, this was undoubtedly a comforting message.

As you prepare for sleep this evening, meditate on the faithfulness of God. What events in your life have more clearly revealed His faithfulness? As you think about these things, remember that because of your relationship to God through Christ Jesus, God is on your side. He will never waver in His devotion and loyalty to you.

Lost and Found

I made your rebellious acts disappear like a thick cloud and your sins like the morning mist. Come back to me, because I have reclaimed you.

Isaiah 44:22

Few things in a child's life are as scary as getting separated from a parent in a public place. When you were young, did the temptation of something interesting ever lure your attention away from following a grown-up? Temporarily enthralled, you lost sight of your parent, so fixed you were on that diversion. But after the luster eventually wore off, you looked up and were horrified to find that your authority, guide, and source of everything was gone.

Sometimes your faith walk may feel like that. You get distracted from the straight path and then one day realize you've lost sight of the One leading your journey. But take heart. The Lord reclaims you. Consider the situation described in Isaiah 44. The people of Israel had strayed from the path. But God promised to reclaim His people.

He continually pursues you. He's there waiting for you to come back to Him when you get off track. It is at that point that God sends your wanderlust scooting away with the wind and your diversions dissipate into thin air.

In the hustle and bustle of your daily life, you can feel His redeeming presence. When things get stressful today, remember His soothing love. He's there with you, reclaiming you, wooing you, His true love. Can you hear Him?

Ways to Pray

*Pray in the Spirit in every situation. Use every kind of prayer
and request there is. For the same reason be alert. Use every kind
of effort and make every kind of request for all of God's people.*

Ephesians 6:18

There are so many different ways to communicate with others. We
can call or send an email, a telegram, a fax, or a text message. But
when the phone lines are down or your internet service provider
is experiencing technical problems, communication is difficult.

In his letter to the Ephesian believers, the apostle Paul encouraged another kind of communication: prayer. The Holy Spirit is
the means for this form of communication. Since He lives within
each believer, we don't have to depend on technology to communicate with Him.

Nighttime is a great time to explore different ways to express
yourself to God. Tonight, try praying in a different way than you
usually do. If you usually speak your prayers to God, try singing to
Him. If you usually pray on your knees, pray standing up instead.
God is relational, and He wants an intimate relationship with you.
Talking to God is a beautiful way to grow in intimacy with Him.

As you pray to God tonight, you don't need to use fancy words
or spiritual-sounding phrases. Ask the Holy Spirit to help you
express your heart to God and connect with God's heart. You can
also request His help and blessing for others. Enjoy communing
with the Creator of the Universe, who loves you.

Dry Places, Dry Times

The LORD will continually guide you and satisfy you even in sun-baked places. He will strengthen your bones. You will become like a watered garden and like a spring whose water does not stop flowing.

Isaiah 58:11

Death Valley National Park in California is one of the hottest places on earth and holds the record for the highest temperature ever recorded in the United States (134° Fahrenheit in 1913). It typically receives less than three inches of rain per year.

Even if you haven't experienced Death Valley in person, you have likely experienced periods of drought where you live. Withered crops, brown lawns, and water rationing accompany times when the rainfall is less than usual.

Dry places and times can happen in your spiritual life as well. There are seasons when it may feel as if you're trudging through a lonely, barren landscape rather than experiencing the fruitful life Jesus promised His followers. Perhaps you've tried (and failed) to navigate your way out of this time of drought.

The prophet Isaiah understood both physical and spiritual deserts. He also understood the character of God. Isaiah's words proclaiming God's promise of abundant life echo today across your desert experience. Today God is inviting you to trust Him right where you are, and allow Him to supernaturally guide and nourish you so you will bloom like a beautiful garden in that parched place.

Intentionally Stubborn

With perfect peace you will protect those whose minds cannot be changed, because they trust you. Trust the LORD always, because the LORD, the LORD alone, is an everlasting rock.

Isaiah 26:3–4

In our culture, if you refuse to change your mind about something, others may think that you are stubborn, old-fashioned, or even rude. We live in a world where many people do not have strong convictions and, therefore, change their minds as easily as they change their shoes.

But there is something worth being stubborn about—trusting in God! This verse in Isaiah speaks of how those who trust in the Lord have minds that "cannot be changed" because they are fixed on trusting their God. They're like photographs—fixed forever at a certain point. So, why do they "stubbornly" trust? Because the Lord is "an everlasting rock," the one who never changes and can, therefore, always be trusted.

If it seems that you have been pressured to change your mind about trusting in the Lord, now is the time to set your trust in Him again. Yes, the world may change, but God's love and care for you never will. So before going to sleep tonight, take a few moments to focus on God and choose to trust in Him again. When you have your mind set on one thing above all others—trusting God—you will experience a perfect peace that comes from heaven.

The God Bag

So don't ever worry about tomorrow. After all, tomorrow will worry about itself. Each day has enough trouble of its own.

Matthew 6:34

Our thoughts as we begin the day sometimes set the tone for how the day progresses. At times the day barely gets under way before we begin worrying about its outcome. Are you full of regret for the past or dread for the future? In these verses, Jesus teaches the futility of worry. Yet worry seems to be hardwired into human nature. It is a very difficult habit to break, but it can be done.

The secret of success is to find a practical way to release your fears and worries to the Lord so that you know you really have given Him your problems.

How can you do that? Here's a suggestion. It may seem silly, but it works. Take a paper lunch bag and write My God Bag on it. Next, write on slips of paper anything that has been troubling you: a problem at work, an argument with your spouse, worries over your children, fear of the future. Write each as a prayer to God and ask for His help. Be as specific as you can. Date each slip, sign it, then fold it up and put it in the bag.

The next time you are tempted to worry, you will remember that you have given it to God in a tangible act of faith. You have done all you can—now let it go, and let God work. In His time and in His way, God will take care of you.

Light in the Darkness

Darkness now covers the earth, and thick darkness covers the nations. But the LORD dawns, and his glory appears over you.

Isaiah 60:2

Storms at night seem to hold more menace. Some of the worst storms in history—Hurricane Katrina, for example—have taken place at night. Even though nightfall already eclipses the light, the added layer of darkness seems to add to the oppression. Is it any wonder that a lighthouse is such a symbol of hope during such a stormy time? You can just picture the beam of light piercing the gloom and helping a storm-tossed ship to navigate to safety.

In Isaiah 60:2, the prophet Isaiah talks about a different sort of darkness: spiritual darkness. After predicting the future exile of the people of Israel, Isaiah then contrasts the glory of the Lord, which the people of Israel were to reflect, with the darkness of the earth. While Israel often failed to reflect God's glory (hence the exile), God would show them great mercy. Through them would come the ultimate light—the Messiah. This light would pierce the darkness—showing the way to God.

What storms have come your way? Perhaps you feel misunderstood, confused about an event in your life, or fearful about an outcome. Perhaps you even question God's concern for your life. If so, consider the message of this verse from Isaiah. The glory of the Lord as embodied in Jesus, "the light of the world" (John 8:12), illuminates the darkness. No darkness can conquer you, because He is your keeper.

Morning Priority

In the morning, long before sunrise, Jesus went to a place where he could be alone to pray.

Mark 1:35

In the pitch black of early morning, Jesus awoke and silently slipped off by Himself. He urgently wanted to seek God, and to find a quiet place without distractions where He could talk and listen.

It's mysterious, isn't it? That Jesus would need to pray to His heavenly Father? In one of His prayers right before His death, we catch a glimpse of the relationship between Father and Son as Jesus was on this earth: "I have given [my followers] the glory that you gave me. I did this so that they are united in the same way we are. I am in them, and you are in me. So they are completely united. In this way the world knows that you have sent me and that you have loved them in the same way you have loved me" (John 17:22–23).

Jesus and the Father were one, yet Jesus needed the constant intimate fellowship of time with the Father. And because Jesus prayed that way, you too are one with your heavenly Father through the Holy Spirit. He is in you.

Like Jesus, you have set aside some quiet time this morning to seek God. You know that today is like a locked door and only your heavenly Father knows what's behind it. You will soon get dressed and step through today's door, so you know how important it is to first sit and talk with the One who knows what this day holds.

Every Season

If any of you are having trouble, pray. If you are happy, sing psalms.

James 5:13

Every one of us will go through different seasons in life—seasons of joy, seasons of sorrow, seasons of trouble, seasons of rest. How we relate to God during those different seasons in life will change as we are shaped by the events of a season. This verse in James acknowledges these differences and even instructs us how to react when we face different seasons.

How are you feeling tonight? Whether you are happy or sad, exuberant or troubled, you can always come to God. If you are troubled tonight, you may find it hard to sing songs of praise. God understands. You can pray in your trouble, though, even if all you can do is ask God for help and rest. He will hear you—and you will not be in this season forever.

If you are full of happiness tonight, sing your joy to God. He loves your voice and created you to praise Him with your lips. So whether you turn music on and sing along to praise songs or create a song in your heart for God, delight in Him and His goodness toward you. He is worthy of our praise!

God knows your heart and longs to connect with you, whether through prayer or song. Take some time to connect with God in the way that expresses your heart to Him tonight, and sleep with the deep peace of a woman who knows her Maker.

Riding Out the Storm

Then he got up and ordered the wind and the waves to stop.
The wind stopped, and the sea became calm. He asked them,
"Where is your faith?"

Luke 8:24–25

Imagine the scene: a small fishing boat tossed like a bottle in the churning waves. The fishermen fear they will be swamped at any minute. Do you blame them for being afraid? And yet Jesus asks them, "Where is your faith?"

This is probably not the question that the disciples would have expected in the middle of a terrifying storm. But Jesus had a point to prove. It was all about where the disciples were looking: at the waves instead of at Jesus.

Your Father wants you to trust Him in the midst of the tempest, when it seems that the hurricane will sweep your home out to sea and when the gale is about to flood your tiny boat.

When storms begin to test your strength, do not be ashamed of being afraid. Jesus' disciples were afraid, and they had Jesus with them in their boat! Learn from them and take a moment to ask yourself, "Where is my faith?" Have you put your faith in your own abilities or in another person, so that suddenly it seems shaky and on the verge of collapse? Relax! You can ride out the storm. You have Jesus in your boat.

This morning, remember that when storms blow into your life, your Father, who has power over wind and waves, will protect you. Have faith. Your Father is with you in the storm. He will bring calm.

Set Free!

Come to me, all who are tired from carrying heavy loads, and I will give you rest.

Matthew 11:28

You know what it's like to feel bone weary. At the end of a hard day, all you want to do is sink into a chair or lie down. But too often, exhaustion is a constant companion. Tired from the events of busy days, you slip into bed feeling the weight of the world on your shoulders. Not only are you bone weary physically but also emotionally. There are always more things to be done, and there never seem to be enough hours in the day to complete the tasks in front of you. You look to sleep to escape the heavy problems that you carry.

Thankfully, Jesus tells you that you do not have to carry these burdens on your own. He calls you to Himself, declaring that when you are tired from shouldering too much in your life, He will give you the rest that you need. More than just sleep, the rest that Christ offers is a rest for your soul (Matthew 11:29), one that refreshes you from the inside out.

Before your head hits the pillow tonight, take some time to tell Jesus about the burdens that are weighing you down emotionally, physically, and spiritually. Then, ask Him for the rest that He offers. You can fall asleep trusting Him to refresh and renew your soul.

The Right Choice

The Lord answered her, "Martha, Martha! You worry and fuss about a lot of things. There's only one thing you need. Mary has made the right choice, and that one thing will not be taken away from her."

Luke 10:41–42

As you read this passage this morning, perhaps you're not surprised that human nature has changed so little over the centuries. Most women today can relate to Martha rather than to Mary. Somehow the urgent still seems to always overshadow the important. Maybe this morning, by the time you get to this, you've already done a load of laundry, washed some dishes, vacuumed the rug, and mopped the floor. Perhaps you have a list of other tasks as well that seem to require your immediate attention.

Jesus is not saying that these tasks aren't important. They are necessary for taking care of your family and home. Nevertheless, He's concerned about your heart. Martha probably thought she made the right choice. After all, wasn't she hard at work to prepare a meal for Jesus? But Jesus knew Mary made the better choice. Spending time with Him was more important than serving Him.

This morning, consider the choices before you. The Bible promises that everyday necessities such as food, clothes, homes, and chores will be provided by seeking Jesus first, and spending time with Him (see Matthew 6:33). Try it this morning and see if your day doesn't flow more easily and productively.

Guard Your Heart

Guard your heart more than anything else, because the source of your life flows from it.

Proverbs 4:23

What flows from your heart? Praise? Complaints? Oftentimes, the deepest desires of our hearts come out as we prepare to sleep. In the Bible, the heart is often used as a metaphor for the core of a person's personality. It is our "source of life." Our actions and thoughts begin at our source, which is our hearts. And that is precisely why the wise writer Solomon told his sons to guard their hearts. Because the heart is the source of life, it needs to be protected from all that would potentially pollute it.

Jesus says that "your heart will be where your treasure is" (Matthew 6:21). Whatever we set our hearts on becomes the treasure—the priority or focus—of our lives. If we claim God as the source of our lives, that means He is the highest priority of our lives. Everything—the relationships we form, the activities we choose, the images we view—flows from that source. Thus, He invites us to guard our hearts from the pollution of worldly ideas and actions. We can do this by saying no to certain images or thoughts and saying yes to sources that accord with God's viewpoint.

Starting tonight, determine to guard your heart. The good news is that you don't have to go it alone. The Holy Spirit is with you to help safeguard His home—your heart. The best way to begin guarding your heart is to give it fully to Him.

A Joyful Command

Arise! Shine! Your light has come, and the glory of the LORD has dawned.

Isaiah 60:1

"Arise! Shine!" What a command! But this is not a command to be perky in the morning even if you don't feel like it. Through His command to Israel, the Lord encourages you to be filled with joy because His presence is in all things.

In Isaiah 60, the God of Israel makes great promises concerning Jerusalem. After His people experienced decades of exile and the city of Jerusalem invaded and destroyed, there would someday be a great homecoming. Many would return to Jerusalem, and every nation would someday flock to the city by land and sea to enrich it. And most wonderful of all, the prophet Isaiah explained, "The Lord will be your everlasting light. Your God will be your glory" (Isaiah 60:19).

Perhaps you're going through a devastating time when the command to "Arise! Shine!" seems impossible to obey. But there is good news: God can bring abundance out of devastation. Joy comes as a result of God's action ("the glory of the Lord has dawned"). This morning, remember the Father's incredible promises for the future. "The glory of the Lord has dawned." He is with you and loves you. "Arise! Shine!"

Splendor All Around

*The sun has one kind of splendor, the moon has another kind
of splendor, and the stars have still another kind of splendor.
Even one star differs in splendor from another star.*

1 Corinthians 15:41

Paul wrote to the people of Corinth to inspire them with the
glory promised to Christ's followers. As they struggled with the
notion of a resurrected body, the Corinthians probably wondered
whether or not their sick, aging bodies would continue troubling
them in heaven.

Perhaps you have the same question tonight as you consider
aches of the day. The images of splendor that Paul provides can
be reassuring. Heaven means perfection. The body you will have
in eternity will never grow old. In fact, the promise of resurrection
is that you will be lit with splendor and experience a new kind
of freedom. It's like the leaves of the hollyhock. They may look
rough and unappealing as the plant grows, but nothing compares
to the beauty of the flowers.

There is a purpose and a plan to this universe! Tonight you
can look out your windows to see how the night sky shimmers
with wonder. If God showers such beauty and abundance on the
fields and in the sky, He must love you dearly.

Such a wonderful pattern you have to ponder. The world has
been painted with designs to remind you—day follows night,
freedom from pain comes with sleep, and the resurrection will
bring splendor that will last throughout eternity.

At a Loss for Words

I saw the glory of the God of Israel coming from the east. His voice was like the sound of rushing water, and the earth was shining because of his glory.

Ezekiel 43:2

Have you ever tried to describe something or someone only to find that you simply can't find the right words, no matter how hard you try? Perhaps you've wished for a bigger vocabulary or the creativity to paint a more vivid word picture as you tried to describe a beautiful patch of sky or a majestic river.

This above Scripture passage finds prophet Ezekiel experiencing the limits of language in a very profound way. The Lord had been showing Ezekiel the beauty of the place of worship He was calling His people Israel to create, right down to the dimensions of this breathtaking temple. But as Ezekiel's vision of the temple came to a conclusion, the limitless God came and filled the temple with His presence. Ezekiel reached for the right words, comparing God's glory to a brilliant sunrise, and the sound of His voice to roaring water.

The very next verse tells us what happened to Ezekiel in his vision of God filling the temple: "This vision was like the one I saw when he came to destroy Jerusalem and like the one I saw by the Chebar River. I immediately bowed down" (43:3). Ezekiel had no words to describe the indescribable God.

Today, the Lord is still filling His temple, you, with His presence. Worship Him for all that He is. And then continue to worship Him, even when you run out of words to describe His beauty and majesty.

Curl Up and Rest

This is what the Almighty LORD, the Holy One of Israel, says:
You can be saved by returning to me. You can have rest. You
can be strong by being quiet and by trusting me.

Isaiah 30:15

A small baby curled up in the crib. Your dog or cat sprawled on the rug, sound asleep. What a picture of rest.

The prophet Isaiah describes another picture of rest: the security and peace inherent in placing the full weight of one's trust in God. Repentance was the step to attaining this security. However, the people of Judah clung to their old ways or repeatedly looked for help from other nations instead of trusting God.

God invites you to put the whole weight of your trust in Him as well and indulge in toe-curling rest. Even when you stray, God gives you opportunities to turn back to Him again and again. And what's more—He will give you rest, peace, and comfort. He'll give you everything you need to get through the tribulations of your life.

Isn't it reassuring to know that you don't have to muster up superhuman strength to fight all of life's battles? Instead you can turn now, this very night, to God. When you quiet your mind and place your trust in Him, rest comes easily. You can curl up and let go of all your troubles because the source of strength is here. In the stillness of the night, turn to the Holy One.

Below the Surface

*Let's learn about the LORD. Let's get to know the LORD. He will
come to us as sure as the morning comes. He will come to us like
the autumn rains and the spring rains that water the ground.*

Hosea 6:3

Are you a people-watcher? It can be fun to sit and conjecture
about the individuals walking by. You might observe, "That man
is very well dressed, but he doesn't carry himself with much
confidence." Or, "That girl must be very proud of her body, she's
showing so much of it!"

These first-glance superficial speculations are just that—pure
speculation. That well-dressed man may have just finished a bad
interview. The scantily clad teen might be seeking attention she's
not getting at home. The truth is, it's difficult to learn much at
all about people—especially what's in their hearts—based on a
surface encounter.

The same is true with God. This verse from Hosea reveals a
surface-level attempt at returning to the Lord. The people hoped
to manipulate God into giving them His favor. But God was not
fooled. A superficial relationship will not reveal His heart. He has
a profoundly deep and wonderful bond planned between the two of
you, but knowing Him personally is foundational for it to develop.

Has God seemed distant or unreliable lately? Consider whether
you have been spending time learning at the feet of the Teacher.
Cultivating a cherished rapport with the Master opens the gate for
Him to become as dependable as the seasonal rains and sunrise.
Tuck that promise away in your own heart this morning as you
open it up to mingle with His.

Hide-and-Seek

When you look for me, you will find me. When you whole-heartedly seek me, I will let you find me, declares the LORD.

Jeremiah 29:13–14

Remember playing hide-and-seek as a kid? The shivering excitement of hiding and seeking is great as the game goes, but not so fun when the game becomes reality. For example, when answers to prayer seem a long time in coming, we sometimes feel as if God is hiding from us just as we're seeking Him.

Nevertheless, the Old Testament prophet Jeremiah provides an assurance of God's willingness to be found. If we seek God wholeheartedly, we will find Him—sometimes in unexpected ways. He can be discovered in the elegance of a sunset, the flickering of a candle flame, and in the gentle breeze coming through the window. And He can be discovered even closer than that. When we truly seek, we will hear the quiet voice of the Holy Spirit inside us. He has been waiting all this time to be found! The key is to keep seeking Him. As Jesus later said, "The one who searches will find, and for the one who knocks, the door will be opened" (Matthew 7:8).

Tonight as you pray, consider the ways God has guided you to this point in your life. Recalling the times of His intervention in your life is a little bit like playing hide-and-seek. Can you find God in your life? He's not hard to find, because He wants you to be found. What a comfort that is.

Wings of the Wind

O LORD my God, you are very great. . . . You stretch out the heavens as though they were curtains. You lay the beams of your home in the water. You use the clouds for your chariot. You move on the wings of the wind.

Psalm 104:1–3

Imagine the job of describing God on paper. How would you do it? How could you capture the beauty, the mercy, the awesome power, and omnipresence of Almighty God in black print on a sheet of white paper?

David tried to do just that. As a prolific psalm writer, he took on the daunting task of describing God in the words of a song. The result is a psalm now numbered 104 in our Bibles. In words that soar across creation, he pictured God clothed with light as with a robe, His home adorned with the heavens as curtains and built with beams set in the vast ocean. He saw God racing across the clouds in a chariot, moving on the wings of the wind.

Exquisite imagery.

As you read the words of this psalm, try to picture the God David describes. Then think about how you would describe God. Who is He to you? A humble Servant, a loving Father, a powerful King? How do you picture Him as you close your eyes to talk with Him? What do you feel when you draw close to Him?

Whatever picture you have of God will be imperfect at best but, like David, you can rejoice in Him, for you know that He is "very great." And that's all you need to be able to join David in singing His praises.

Never Alone

I will not leave you all alone. I will come back to you.

John 14:18

Nighttime often stirs up feelings of loneliness. With the darkness blanketing everything and everyone, we feel isolated, especially if we're the only one awake in the house. But wakefulness isn't only an isolator. It is often an indicator of unresolved problems, fears, and other worries. We feel all alone in our anguish.

If you experienced such a feeling recently, you can understand how Jesus' disciples felt when their beloved Master announced His upcoming death. The One they walked with, ate with, and poured their lives into would be gone. But Jesus also promised that they wouldn't be left alone. Not only would Jesus return from the dead, He also would send the Holy Spirit to be with them always.

Although the disciples couldn't quite grasp Jesus' words at the time, His resurrection (John 20) and the sending of the Holy Spirit (Acts 2) showed that Jesus kept His promise.

This promise is for you as well. Even when you feel troubled and alone, Jesus promises that you are never truly alone. You have the assurance of the Holy Spirit's presence, guidance, comfort, and strength.

Tonight you can rest in the Spirit who surrounds you with love and promises never to leave you. Thanks to the Holy Spirit, you'll never walk alone.

A World Full of Praise

From where the sun rises to where the sun sets, the name of the
LORD should be praised.

Psalm 113:3

The entire earth praising the Lord—what a beautiful picture!
Imagine everyone on the planet joining together to praise the
Lord! At times it seems impossible, yet God has already promised
that someday this will be a reality. Paul explained that one day
"at the name of Jesus everyone in heaven, on earth, and in the
world below will kneel and confess that Jesus Christ is Lord to
the glory of God the Father" (Philippians 2:10–11). In Revelation,
John records his amazing vision when he "heard every creature in
heaven, on earth, under the earth, and on the sea. Every creature
in those places was singing, 'To the one who sits on the throne
and to the lamb be praise, honor, glory, and power forever and
ever'" (Revelation 5:13).

Praise is the language of heaven. Praise pulls you out from
under any burdens you carry today and focuses your thoughts on
God—the One who "bends down to look at heaven and earth. He
lifts the poor from the dust. He lifts the needy from a garbage
heap" (Psalm 113:6–7).

Perfect unity before God is coming! You will be a part of
that incredible time of worship! Begin praising the Father today
in anticipation of that wonderful day when all heaven and earth
unites to praise the Lord. Praise Him today for His plans for you.
Praise Him for the blessings He has given you, big and little. And
most of all, praise Him for His own sake, for being the incredible
Abba, Father, Lord, Almighty God that He is!

Rescue Me

O LORD my God, I have taken refuge in you. Save me, and rescue me from all who are pursuing me.

Psalm 7:1

Sometimes an endless tirade of guilt or recriminations plays in our heads. We toss and turn with messages like *I said the wrong thing. I'm worthless. My mistakes are unforgivable.* At other times the tirade includes the remarks or opinions of others—opinions that rob us of our sleep or cause us to beat ourselves up.

David, the author of this psalm, was accused of trying to steal Saul's throne. While the accusation was untrue, David suffered for it with Saul's relentless pursuit. Rather than seeking revenge, he turned to God for relief.

What is the safest place you can think of? Is it a mountain castle or fortress? Or is your place of refuge someplace closer to home, like a basement—your retreat when storms brew outside? As David explained, there is no safer place than God. He is the ultimate refuge.

The Father's loving arms are stretched out waiting for you to run to Him. When you are in need of a salve for your heart, all you have to do is rush to Him and surrender your life into His powerful care. Like a life preserver, He surrounds you and lifts you to safety.

Surrender isn't a bad thing in this case. It means going to the One who is stronger and wiser and saying, "I need You." Through prayer you can give your doubts to Him. Then in the safety of His arms, the accusations cease. With untroubled thoughts, sleep comes readily.

Immeasurable!

How precious are your thoughts concerning me, O God! How vast in number they are! If I try to count them, there would be more of them than there are grains of sand. When I wake up, I am still with you.

Psalm 139:17–18

We are earthbound, finite creations, aren't we? Even when we purpose to pursue God with a single focus, we are easily distracted by dozens of daily concerns, tasks, and random thoughts. By very definition, our humanity limits us.

Not so with God. He did not create you then decide to shun you because of your limitations. He is always, always, always thinking of you! When David first sang the words to this morning's worship song, he reached for the most immeasurable image in his experience—an endless beach with countless grains of sand—to describe God's unceasing attention on him. He basked in the reality that the number of God's thoughts for him was incalculable.

This is your reality as well. Thank Him for His undivided attention on you and you alone. And bask in His limitless love for you this morning. He is with you here . . . now . . . and always.

Take a bit of time to interact with this powerful passage of Scripture. Read it aloud a couple of times, then bookmark your place, close this book, and ponder as deeply as you can what God is saying to you through His Word this morning. Thank Him that when you awoke this morning, He was with you. Thank Him for His constant thoughts of you.

Shifting Gears

On the day I was in trouble, I went to the Lord for help. At night I stretched out my hands in prayer without growing tired. Yet, my soul refused to be comforted.

Psalm 77:2

Picture it: you've just had a hard day, a day in which you heard some devastating news. You come home and your family tries to cheer you up or comfort you in some way. Could you accept the comfort extended?

When Asaph, the writer of Psalm 77, found himself in anguish, he turned to a tried-and-true source of comfort: God. Yet he still found himself comfortless. By the end of Psalm 77, however, he came to a feeling of acceptance. Meditating on "the deeds of the Lord" (77:11) helped him shift gears.

When you stop seeing God and get stuck in a world of personal troubles, it's hard to find peace of mind. The answer is to switch gears. But this is easier said than done. It can be difficult to shift from your disappointments and expectations to seeing how God works for good.

As you prepare for bed this evening, make that transition from worry to peace by focusing on images of God. Consider how many wonderful people God has brought into your life. How many opportunities has God given you to learn and grow? You can cultivate a feeling of gratitude, and this will lead to courage and change.

To prepare for sleep tonight, try to release your troubles. Shift the focus from me to He. May you then find comfort.

Join the Picnic

A cheerful heart has a continual feast.
Proverbs 15:15

Food brings people together. Add a beautiful summer day, a basket filled with scrumptious food, and a checkered tablecloth and you've got yourself a picnic party! Add a few relatives and friends bringing their own homemade specialties, some laughing children taking fingerfuls of the frosting from the yet-to-be-cut cake, and you're in for a regular feast.

A summer picnic is like that, a continual feast stretching well into the evening when the food is gone and the sun begins to set. People linger over that last bit of lemonade and those few final stories yet to be told.

That's what a cheerful heart looks like. Solomon, the wisest king who ever lived, understood that being cheerful allows a person to live as if every day is a picnic. Looking on the bright side of life helps you appreciate the small blessings, the simple things. Cheerfulness does not have to end; it can go on and on, giving you joy for today and tomorrow, joy that fills your life to overflowing. This kind of cheer is a wonderful trait to pass on to the next generation.

Step up to the table and fill your plate to overflowing. Ask the Lord today to give you a cheerful heart. Then enjoy the feast!

Rise Up, My Soul

Let my prayer be accepted as sweet-smelling incense in your presence. Let the lifting up of my hands in prayer be accepted as an evening sacrifice.

Psalm 141:2

For hundreds of years, incense has accompanied prayer on its journey to God. Wafts of white smoke curl and dance toward the ceiling. As it rises, the smoke symbolically lifts the prayers out of this earthly realm.

David, the writer of Psalm 141, well knew the use of incense in worship. It was a fit metaphor for his desperate plea, which flowed like the smoke of the incense.

The rising smoke also is an image of our faith. It defies gravity by rising heavenward instead of falling back to earth. When we lift our hands and voices toward God, we defy logic too. While an unbelieving person might say there is no physical presence in the room to hear us, we trust that God hears each word.

Your prayers merge with the prayers of others like whiffs of smoke. You ask for forgiveness for yourself or for others. You offer thanks. You ask for help for your troubled world. You seek guidance.

Tonight, you can make a simple ritual by lighting a candle while you pray. After you pray, blow out the candle and watch the smoke rise. As it rises, your soul will rise up with it, to meet your loving Savior.

New Every Morning

His compassion is never limited. It is new every morning. His faithfulness is great.

Lamentations 3:22–23

Compassion is a profound, active emotion. It has inspired people through the ages to fund hospitals, mission trips, communities damaged from weather, and programs for needy children. Compassion for the lost inspires missionaries to forsake their own desires and live among those with whom they hope to share the gospel. Compassion shows love and care even in the dark times.

This verse in Lamentations appears at the center of a book filled with tears. Jeremiah lamented the destruction of the city of Jerusalem by foreign invaders, an event that occurred because Israel had turned away from God and destruction came just as God had warned. Yet even through this dark time, Jeremiah knew that God's compassion was not limited by the people's sin and disobedience. They could turn back to God and He would return to them. His faithfulness is great.

Every morning you receive a fresh, unlimited supply of His compassion. Isn't it exciting that you can count on your heavenly Father to be dependably compassionate? This morning is your new opportunity to pass on compassion to your family, friends, neighbors, and, yes, even the unloving or unlovable people in life.

The world will be better today because of God's compassion given to the world through you.

Are You Listening?

Samuel was asleep in the temple of the LORD where the ark of God was kept. Then the LORD called Samuel. "Here I am," Samuel responded.

1 Samuel 3:3–4

Daytime is often filled with noises and distractions. It is the time to go, accomplish, and check off the to-do list. But nighttime and its coveted hours meant for rest can be hampered with the replaying of these noises and distractions. Sometimes we're so busy replaying the day that we miss listening for "the quiet, whispering voice" of the Lord (1 Kings 19:12).

In 1 Samuel, the importance of an attitude of listening is revealed in an interaction between God and Samuel, a boy given by his mother Hannah to serve God at the tabernacle. One night, Samuel thought he heard someone call his name. Assuming it was Eli, he hurried to the priest's side. This happened three times. After Eli determined that God was calling Samuel, Eli suggested a humble response: "Speak, Lord. I'm listening" (1 Samuel 3:9).

How would you respond if the Lord called your name? Is your life so busy that you wouldn't be able to hear the Lord if He called you? Or would you recognize His voice like an infant recognizes her mother's soft inflection and touch?

God speaks through His Word, through the Holy Spirit, and through the wise counsel of others. His voice is like the quiet voice of a radio host tuned to the frequency of our hearts. Are you listening?

Fill Your Bucket

Everyone who drinks this water will become thirsty again. But those who drink the water that I will give them will never become thirsty again. In fact, the water I will give them will become in them a spring that gushes up to eternal life.

John 4:13–14

The apostle John records a scene of a woman shunned by society, forced to draw her water from the community well during the hottest hours of the day. She carried her bucket in the blazing heat of the day in order to avoid the gossipers, the enemies, and the scoffers. In this famous scene from Scripture, during a typical trip for water the sinful woman found much, much more. She found her Savior.

Jesus shared the hope of salvation with the woman and gave her a glimpse of what it meant to be a follower of Christ. Even after acknowledging her wrong choices, Jesus revealed the hope of a life with Him. Instead of a simple bucket of murky water from a well, Jesus offered living water—the water of eternal life and the presence of the Holy Spirit. It sustains believers in their toughest moments, bringing refreshment in the driest of days.

Do you need more than a sip of living water today? Is the heat of your past choices burning down like the desert sun? Just like the woman at the well, you too can have confidence that God will be with you—even when you seem to be all alone. Trust in Jesus today, and ask Him to pour out His living water over your life. His water never runs out!

Looking Back

Remember your Creator when the doors to the street are closed,
the sound of the mill is muffled, you are startled at the sound
of a bird, and those who sing songs become quiet.

Ecclesiastes 12:4

What do you usually do when you're feeling nostalgic? Play old songs? Look at old photographs? A feeling of nostalgia often involves taking a glance in the rearview mirror of our lives. Captured images can remind us of a loved one, an event, or a fading memory. Sometimes the recollection is calming, especially if the memory evoked is a happy one.

The writer of Ecclesiastes encouraged a sense of nostalgia in regard to the Creator. At the beginning of the chapter, he encouraged the remembrance of God "when you are young" (12:1). In the rest of the chapter, the descending of night and the changes in season are symbolic of the aging process. In a sense he is saying "Remember the Creator throughout your life."

Meditating on your Creator—remembering His attributes and actions—is a discipline that can carry you through good and bad times. You can ready yourself for taxing moments by consistently preparing and praying. Preparing—reading the Word, seeking wise counsel—equips you as you go through life. If you are grounded in the comfortable moments, you will be more likely to stay grounded in the challenging ones, when it is so much easier to become jaded.

As you lie in bed, consider the ways your Creator made His presence known during your faith journey. How can you continue to equip yourself for a lifelong journey with Christ?

The Good Teacher

The Lord may give you troubles and hardships. But your teacher will no longer be hidden from you. You will see your teacher with your own eyes. You will hear a voice behind you saying, "This is the way. Follow it, whether it turns to the right or to the left."

Isaiah 30:20–21

It may be that the teacher who did not make school easy for you was, in fact, the teacher who gave you the best guidance. She required that you work hard and, in doing so, taught you discipline and perseverance. It is possible that you were not always fond of her; it would have been more comfortable if she had not asked so much of you. Yet years later, as an adult, you look back and appreciate the hard work she did. It showed that she cared about her subject matter—and about you.

Your Father is the greatest of teachers and He wants nothing less than your complete devotion. He cares about His subject matter—and about you. He wants to grow you into the person He created you to be, and usually that requires some long homework assignments and tough tests. And He can be a tough teacher sometimes as He allows pop quizzes of troubles and hardships to come your way. But He does that because He knows that those will be your best lessons; those will help you grow strong as you learn to trust and love Him through it all. He doesn't leave you alone in the difficult times, however. He is the voice behind you offering guidance to help you pass the test.

This morning, tell the Lord you want to be an exemplary student. Thank Him for caring enough to teach you, guide you, walk with you, and love you.

A Place of Rest

He will say to them, "This is a place for comfort. This is a place of rest for those who are tired. This is a place for them to rest."

Isaiah 28:12

You've spent a very busy day. You've worked hard. You've handled your share of excitement, joy, sorrow, crises—you name it. The day is over and now it's time to rest.

What if you decided you weren't going to rest? What if you said that you wanted to keep going, keep working through the night and into the next day? Eventually, your body would overrule and you would collapse into much-needed sleep. Your body knows that you need rest in order to keep up with your responsibilities.

The context of the verse in Isaiah comes as God was speaking to His people in the northern kingdom of Israel. They had sinned greatly. The last phrase of the verse above (not quoted) is "but they weren't willing to listen." Isaiah reminded the people that God had given them the land of Canaan in which to rest, but they took Him for granted and rejected His provision. They had other plans; they wanted to go their own way.

Today's world offers an endless supply of activities and opportunities. When you allow your daily routines to define, control, and deplete you, however, it is an indication that reprioritization is needed. God wants you to rest when you're tired; He knows you need it. Which activities are preventing you from resting? Ask the Lord to help you slow down, reset your priorities, and find the rest that you need.

After all, tomorrow is a busy day.

Light the Path

A new day will dawn on us from above because our God is loving and merciful. He will give light to those who live in the dark and in death's shadow. He will guide us into the way of peace.

Luke 1:78–79

A light shone in the dark forest. The flashlight bobbed up and down along the walking trail as several people followed along behind. Without the light, everyone would have stumbled in the eerie darkness, potentially lost, hurt, and alone. Fortunately, a leader with the bright light guided the group out of the denseness toward safety. As long as the group followed the leader with the light, they stayed safely on the path.

Luke records the story of Zechariah's words as he held his precious son John. The Lord gave Zechariah a prophecy about the future of this promised child. John would become like a brave leader in a dark forest holding out the light that would guide people to safety. He would bring to his people the message that the long-awaited Messiah was coming and the people would find their salvation in Him. Indeed, a new day had dawned.

Do you feel that you're in the dark today, in a time of deep shadow? Does the morning light only barely nudge the darkness from your heart? God can give you light; God can guide you into the way of peace. Ask Him to shine his bright light into the darkness and show you the way through. Then stay right behind Him and follow.

Sensing God

Who among you fears the LORD and obeys his servant? Let those who walk in darkness and have no light trust the name of the LORD and depend upon their God.

Isaiah 50:10

The Lord has given us senses to detect Him. They are tools to know and follow Him. He gave us eyes to see the purple shades of sunsets, noses to smell the deep musk of autumn and lilac springs, ears to hear rain gently spilling onto roofs, tongues to taste fresh produce, and touch to feel the soft sand between our toes.

But isn't it interesting how in sudden dark situations, we feel cut off from some of our senses? The sudden blackout disorients us. Not only can't we see, we're often not sure we hear as well either!

Isaiah used darkness as a metaphor for times of turmoil. During those times when we're tempted to panic or doubt our senses, Isaiah champions a dependence on God. Only He can see all sides of a situation. So, instead of flailing about in the darkness of our misunderstanding, we are to trust in the presence of God. The Holy Spirit is like a spiritual compass—one that always points us in the right direction.

As you lie in bed tonight, focus on each of your senses and how they may be used to acknowledge the Lord and strengthen your faith. Revisit your day. When did you use your senses to recognize the Lord or to further the kingdom? In what tangible ways did He help you when you were tempted to doubt your senses?

A "God Boost"

Everything written long ago was written to teach us so that we would have confidence through the endurance and encouragement which the Scriptures give us.

Romans 15:4

If you're still sleepy-eyed from a night's sleep that ended far too soon, reach for a "God boost." Grab your Bible and a cup of hot tea, and settle into your most comfy chair. See what the Lord wants to reveal to you through His Word today.

God has given you a wonderful book of promises and encouragement, written centuries ago and inspired by the Holy Spirit, as the apostle Paul explains. Faithful servants of the Lord wrote, studied, and protected the Scriptures throughout the ages, making sure you would have a copy to read today. The Bible is God's living love letter to you. It is alive (see Hebrews 4:12) and packed full of captivating stories and meaningful insight that applies to your daily life. His Word speaks to your generation, even in a world full of cell phones, the internet, and a vast array of technological distractions.

God's Word gives you confidence to live each day dedicated to Him and the grace to be in loving relationship with His Son, Jesus Christ. The Bible bears witness to who Jesus is and who you are in Him. What better way to begin the day with a heightened sense of who God is than to read the Scriptures!

Make-Believe

So don't ever worry about tomorrow. After all, tomorrow will worry about itself. Each day has enough trouble of its own.

Matthew 6:34

An old pair of high heels, one of grandmother's fancy party hats, and a mismatched collection of bangle bracelets beckon most little girls into whimsical fairy tales, imaginary worlds, and fantastic daydreams. Cares and concerns, although seemingly simple in childhood, are whisked away as each bracelet slips over a tiny wrist and an elegant lady, bedecked in costume jewelry, emerges. No adventure is out of bounds, no dream impossible. Reality will wait until costumes and jewelry are returned to their cluttered toy trunk at the end of the day.

As today comes to an end, which aspects of reality and its trials surface and consume you? Do you wish that an assortment of once-polished bracelets could be slipped on, allowing you to escape to that perfectly painted setting? Take heart. In Christ, dress-up clothes or an escape into fantasy are not necessary for solace. Instead, He offers true solace by cautioning His followers to avoid worrying about what will happen tomorrow. This is not a bury-your-head-in-the-sand piece of advice, but an invitation to lay your worries and burdens down at His feet. As the Lord points out, "Can any of you add a single hour to your life by worrying?" (Matthew 6:27). Instead, you can trust in the Lord; trust in His promises. His faithfulness will never lose its luster.

Access to Abundance

We have the mind of Christ.
1 Corinthians 2:16

The computer is a marvel of technology. The colossal amount of information available is more than anyone could ever use. Tidbits and data details, history and scientific minutia, trivia beyond imagination or usefulness, world encyclopedias at your fingertips—all thanks to the internet.

If you think about it long enough, the quantity of information could boggle your mind. But can you imagine how much more detail God has in His mind? More than all the data in this universe, He knows absolutely everything. He knows the number of hairs on the heads of the world's nearly seven billion people, the exact nanosecond of each person's birth, and even the number of molecules in the oceans. Wow! He holds every minute detail about everything.

Amazingly, you have access to Christ's abundance of knowledge. All you have to do is connect to the source. Log on. Be in touch.

If you are faced with a decision or a difficult problem, you do not have to solve it by yourself. Talk to Jesus about it. He has more information than you have and can help you find answers to any dilemma in life. You have the mind of Christ.

A Renewed Soul

He makes me lie down in green pastures. He leads me beside peaceful waters. He renews my soul.

Psalm 23:2–3

As you sit down in the evening and exhale that deep, end-of-day exhalation, imagine yourself sitting on the edge of a wooden dock at sunset. You experience creation's quiet magnificence. When you dip your toes into the calming water, weariness is eased and rest is found. When the sultry breeze brushes through your hair and you listen to the ebbing tide breaking across the shore, peace is found. When your eyes follow the setting sun's golden trail across the water's glassy surface and into the hills, restoration is found.

The Lord desires rest and restoration for His children. David, the onetime shepherd turned king of Israel, recognized God as a shepherd who cares for His flock. He commands us to, "Let go of your concerns! Then you will know that I am God" (Psalm 46:10). Christ provides us with settings that promise stillness. He guides us into havens that encourage comfort. He desires us to seek and secure moments of rest so that our souls might be renewed. A tranquil soul is a soul that is capable of serving and worshiping the Creator.

As you lie in bed tonight, ask the Lord to quiet your soul so that you might reflect on Him and wake rested and revitalized tomorrow.

What's Your Foundation?

People may build on this foundation with gold, silver, precious stones, wood, hay, or straw. The day will make what each one does clearly visible because fire will reveal it. That fire will determine what kind of work each person has done.

1 Corinthians 3:12–13

A building needs a strong foundation in order to hold the structure together. If the foundation is weak, the building will collapse.

What is the foundation of your life? Where do your values, hopes, dreams, ideas, and inspiration originate? Consider this passage written by the apostle Paul. Here, he is talking about motivation. If Jesus is foundational to your life, then He is present with you. This affects everything you do. All your effort and energy will pass the test of time because He guides you to make choices consistent with His principles. But it is your choice to make—either to live by His rules or by your own ideas.

At the end of life, will you wish for a nicer house, more fashionable clothes, and a fancier car? Or will you be happy knowing you have cultivated relationships with family and friends, and that you tried in your own way to spread God's love wherever you went?

As is the case with tempering gold, some works will burn up in the fires of testing and blow away, leaving nothing of substance behind in which to add to a spiritual foundation. But those who choose to spend their time wisely will leave a legacy of changed hearts and lives by sharing Jesus.

How will you add to the foundation of life? The choice is yours.

Tucked In

He will cover you with his feathers, and under his wings you will find refuge. His truth is your shield and armor. You do not need to fear terrors of the night, arrows that fly during the day, plagues that roam the dark.

Psalm 91:4–6

For children, nighttime often inspires a range of far-fetched notions and menacing fears, some of which are alleviated when a parent arrives to tuck them in and assure them that everything is okay. For adults, dark shadows no longer unleash a fury of monsters and apprehensions, but life's day-to-day challenges do. Sickness, financial instability, job struggles, concern for children—these occur day and night. We long for someone to take away our fears or pain—to tuck us in, so to speak, with words of comfort.

Can you relate? If so, consider the message of Psalm 91 and its vivid images of protection and provision. We need not fear the trials of this life because God, who is our protection and harbor, covers us. He has given us the Holy Spirit to dwell inside us as we learn and grow from the challenges we encounter. He also has given us His Word as a guide to truth.

As you crawl into bed at night, contemplate the ways in which the Lord looks after you. Perhaps He provided wise counsel at just the right time. Or, perhaps He flooded you with peace as you waited for the doctor's diagnosis. Tonight, allow the truth of His love for you to tuck you in. You can rest assured under His wings.

Stay Put

So, then, brothers and sisters, don't let anyone move you off the foundation of your faith. Always excel in the work you do for the Lord. You know that the hard work you do for the Lord is not pointless.

1 Corinthians 15:58

Wanting to encourage the Corinthian believers, Paul reminded them to excel in their efforts. Apparently, it was just as easy in Paul's day to put forth the bare minimum effort needed. But Christians are called to a higher standard of excellence.

What would this look like today? Although the circumstances of life are different from Paul's time, the two basic principles remain the same. First, excel in whatever work you do for the Lord today. It's not as complicated as it may sound. One way is to think back to the two commands of Jesus in Matthew 22:37–40: love God and love your neighbor. Is your work today for love of God or the good of another? Excellence means doing the loving thing.

Second, ask yourself what is the next right thing to do? This is a question to take to the Lord for His input. The world constantly tries to press its values on you, to sway you to thoughts of materialism, self-importance, greed, or pride. Remember that excellence means doing the next right thing and not buying into wrong values. It takes a conscious choice to keep Jesus' commands uppermost in mind and to stay put with Him. This choice must be made fresh each morning. Like a puppy learning to obey his owner, you can read God's Word and find out exactly how He wants you to love Him and love others.

It really is that simple.

Seal of Approval

Now that we have God's approval by faith, we have peace with God because of what our Lord Jesus Christ has done.

Romans 5:1

Human approval is often based on certain conditions being met. A person might gain our approval through obedience or by possessing a trait we admire (beauty, goodness, success, fame, independence of thought, high intellect). We withhold our approval if the conditions we've set are not met.

In the letter to the Romans, the apostle Paul describes another kind of approval—God's. We can't earn it by being "good." Instead, God approves us "because of what Jesus Christ has done." This means that because of Jesus' perfect fulfillment of every letter of the law and especially His sacrificial death on the cross, we are no longer at war with God. Jesus' resurrection sealed the deal and ushered in a new era of peace with God.

Tonight, consider who or what gains your seal of approval. What are the times when you're most tempted to believe that you don't have God's approval? If your faith has been shaken recently because of a hardship, meditate on Paul's words. Consider also these words from Paul: "I am convinced that nothing can ever separate us from God's love which Christ Jesus our Lord shows us" (Romans 8:38).

Tonight as you close your eyes, consider the amazing fact that you have God's seal of approval.

The Ripple Effect

As all of us reflect the Lord's glory with faces that are not covered with veils, we are being changed into his image with ever-increasing glory. This comes from the Lord, who is the Spirit.

2 Corinthians 3:18

When someone smiles at you, you can't help smiling back. Perhaps that smile spurs you to smile at someone else. That's the ripple effect. Like the ripples in a pond, which start out small and slowly spread over the whole surface, one kind act is all it takes.

So, how do you do this? By faith.

First, trust that God's Spirit is inside you at this very moment, changing you into God's image and making you look and act differently. Second, listen carefully. The Spirit is just waiting for a chance to inspire you. Can you hear even the subtlest whisper? Be still, quiet, and receptive. You might also read all of 2 Corinthians 3. How do Jesus' ways compare to or differ from the ways you normally behave? Can you think of several simple ways to love people you will see today?

You reflect the Spirit of God simply by the love you show to others. Your kindness will yield kindness. And, like a pebble tossed into a pond yields ripples, kindness flows outward from just one simple act, inspiring others.

Turn to the Lord today and ask to be changed. Pay attention and, when you feel a nudge, act on it. Trust that it will set off many more ripples of kindness, blessing many.

Journeying Home

*There will be no more night, and they will not need any light
from lamps or the sun because the Lord God will shine on them.
They will rule as kings forever and ever.*

Revelation 22:5

Have you ever dreamed about taking a trip to a distant, exotic
place? Most of us know what this is like. We long for the opportunity to see new places, to experience something different.
We know such a trip will refresh and renew us.

Could you imagine your own home being a place of refreshment as well as exciting and exotic? Your true home—heaven—is.
We have hints of what this special destination will be like from
the book of Revelation. According to the vision of the apostle
John, it is a place of wonderful illumination. Our eyes will be
able to feast on beautiful golden light. All truth and all reality will
be clear. We will be with the King and live as kings. And there
will be no more death, no more darkness, no more fear. Such a
bountiful place of perfection and purity it will be!

The light of heaven trickles down into our lives now. When
we're confused about choices or challenges, God provides "light"
through His Word to guide us (Psalm 119:105; Ephesians 1:18).

As you prepare for sleep tonight, consider what excites you the
most about this awesome heavenly home. If you've spent all day
in the hot sun or worried about paying your electric bill, perhaps
the thought of never needing another lamp might fill you with
longing. If so, that's great! This dream becomes a beacon during
your journey on earth. Like a spotlight, it points the way home.

Life's Thorns

That problem, Satan's messenger, torments me to keep me from being conceited. I begged the Lord three times to take it away from me. But he told me: "My kindness is all you need. My power is strongest when you are weak."

2 Corinthians 12:7–9

As you wake this morning and start your day, is there something worrying you and stealing away your peace? The apostle Paul daily faced a problem that he called "Satan's messenger" (some translations use the word "thorn").

This was a problem that Paul wanted to be rid of, something that continually bothered him. Though it's not known for sure what this problem was, what is known is that Paul badly wanted relief. Three times he asked God to remove it. But God didn't. God chose to answer his prayer in another, better way. Paul was given something much more important. He learned the gift of acceptance, and discovered that in his acceptance lay Christ's strength and peace.

Today, instead of letting this problem prick you like a thorn, why not try a new way of handling it? Try accepting it. Decide to take what life gives, at this moment, whatever it is. Your thorn doesn't have to deflate you. This is the key to God being able to work His strength into you. At that moment of acceptance, you will begin to feel God's power to deal with the situation. Trust that God will show you, like Paul, a different way to look at the problem. Turn your weakness over to God, again and again if necessary. His strength is available when you stop resisting and start accepting.

A Purpose for Peace

Let Christ's peace control you. God has called you into this peace by bringing you into one body. Be thankful.

Colossians 3:15

Imagine the feeling of being welcomed home by close family and friends after a long trip. Feel the familiar embraces. See the genuine smiles. Hear the tender voices. This is the intimacy that Christ desires for us among our Christian brothers and sisters. This is the feeling of being part of a whole—one that will carry over in heaven.

We are instructed to love one another (Matthew 22:39; John 13:35). The Lord has called us to live in peace with others, reflecting His love. Sadly, some of our interchanges are characterized by arguments, rather than peace. We snipe and gripe, dwell on misunderstandings, or fall into judgmental thoughts of others. Churches have split and relationships have ended over such misunderstandings. Knowing of human nature, Paul included the above admonition to encourage his readers to be controlled by the Holy Spirit—the author of peace and the One who connects all believers. If we allow the Lord's peace to control our tongues and tempers, we will be a reflection of Him.

Perhaps tonight you're in need of peace. There is no better time than now to ask for it.

Shining Armor

*Put on all the armor that God supplies. In this way you can
take a stand against the devil's strategies.*

Ephesians 6:11

Imagine a skier whooshing down the slopes with no coat, gloves,
or ski boots. She would suffer weather damage. What if your
friend was a police officer or a soldier, but refused to wear a bul-
letproof vest while rushing to stop an armed robber or an enemy
attack? You'd probably think she was foolish and asking to get
hurt. After all, injuries can occur when people aren't completely
protected against the outdoor elements or on the job.

The same is true for the Christian. The devil is a powerful, con-
niving enemy who constantly battles against believers. Thankfully
God supplies protection: spiritual armor. This includes God's truth
and approval, the gospel message and a believer's willingness
to spread it, faith, the helmet of salvation, and the sword of the
Spirit—God's Word (Ephesians 6:13–17). The apostle Paul also
suggested prayer as an important part of your battle strategy. With
His armor, you can stand up to your soul's adversary.

Some Christians go through life's battles partially clad with
protective gear and needlessly suffer war wounds. Are you fully
protected? It's never too late to admit you need help to stand
against your enemy. Ask for that help and put on your full armor.

As You Are

We can go to God with bold confidence through faith in Christ.

Ephesians 3:12

Ever think of yourself as limited in some way—too limited to be of use to God? If you feel you lack attributes or resources that others have (higher education; a nice house; a sizable bank account; eloquence in speech and other abilities) or if you've made mistakes in the past, you can't imagine being used by God to build His kingdom. Yet consider the fact that the apostle Paul wrote the letter to the Ephesians while imprisoned in Rome. Little did he know that he would have a great impact for the kingdom during this time.

Although he was a prisoner, Paul considered his position a privilege. After all, he had been chosen by God to share His Good News. And that's the whole point, isn't it—being chosen by God to do the work to which you are called? For this very reason, you can approach the Lord confidently, knowing that His mercies extend to all those who believe the gospel.

Consider the way in which you approach the Lord. Do you come cautiously or boldly? As Paul declares, you can draw near the Lord unencumbered—much like a simple sunflower, exposed and concentrated on the vast heavens above. You can bring your burdens and shortcomings to Christ, knowing that His unconditional love and grace are not just for the sinless and blameless. His love and grace are meant for everyone. As today comes to a close, come to the Lord just as you are.

Imitating the Father

*We ask this so that you will live the kind of lives that prove
you belong to the Lord. Then you will want to please him in
every way as you grow in producing every kind of good work
by this knowledge about God.*

Colossians 1:10

Is there someone whom you deeply admire and try to emulate
because you want to please her? Perhaps that person is an older
sister you looked up to all throughout your childhood or your
mother. What did you do to be like her? Did you dress like her
or talk like her? Did you read the books she loved or listen to her
music? When you care about someone, you study that person and
come to know her well. You try to please her by acting like her
or doing things for her. And it is one of your proudest moments
to be told you are just like her.

In Colossians, Paul explains that his desire for the Colossians
was that they would study God and use their deepening knowledge of Him to emulate Him and please Him with "every kind
of good work." God does not require good works for the sake
of salvation; the good works are the natural outcome of a close
relationship with Him. They are the aspects of a life that "prove
you belong to the Lord."

Seek to imitate the Lord more fervently than you've ever tried
to imitate the person you admire. The day you hear the words
"Good job!" (Matthew 25:21) will be your proudest day. You will
know you have learned to be like the Father.

Telling Time

Jesus Christ is the same yesterday, today, and forever.
Hebrews 13:8

The longcase clock, also known as a grandfather clock, has been a symbol of time since its advent in 1670. You can count on it to chime the quarter hour, half hour, and the hour. Tick. Tock. Gong . . . gong . . . gong. The clock indicates the passage of time, and change is time's companion.

Whether or not invited, unexpected twists and turns permeate our lives. As the old saying goes, change is the only constant in this world. Relationships go through seasons of change, jobs change, and disasters sometimes trigger unexpected changes. This is the nature of a temporary world.

Perhaps tonight you're contemplating or reeling from an unexpected change. If so, take heart. The writer of Hebrews declares that Jesus will never change. When all else seems uncertain, rest assured that our Savior was and is and will forever be constant. We can find trust in and rely on Him, knowing that His promises to us will not falter.

Take a moment to quietly reflect on cherished memories that have remained constant in your life from year to year. Is it the family's chiming grandfather clock in the hallway? Is it a tradition that takes place each holiday season? What remains unchanged, providing a sense of comfort and familiarity? Praise God for the constants and for His presence in every season of life.

Real Faith

Faith assures us of things we expect and convinces us of the existence of things we cannot see. . . . No one can please God without faith. Whoever goes to God must believe that God exists and that he rewards those who seek him.

Hebrews 11:1, 6

Hebrews 11 is often referred to as the faith chapter. Seventeen individuals, the prophets as a group, and an entire nation are praised and remembered for their faith in God. Others are mentioned not by name but by what they endured as a result of their faith.

What is faith, really? Of course you have faith that when you retire for the night you will awaken the next morning. You have faith that your car will get you to work, your kids will take care of you when you're old, and the rental place will always have a movie you want to see.

But where does that get you? Are any of those things actually worth real faith? Isn't there a good chance that none of them will come to pass?

Real faith is knowing with every fiber of your being that what you hope for will actually happen. Even though you can't see it, you are certain of its existence. It is like a life jacket or life preserver that keeps you from sinking when the seas of life are at their roughest.

The people in Hebrews 11 had real faith in God. They believed in God's existence and sought to gain a deeper understanding of Him. Their faith pleased God and He rewarded each one—some while still alive and every one of them when they reached heaven.

Your faith in God is the only thing from this life that will go with you into eternity.

Smooth Sailing

Trust the LORD with all your heart, and do not rely on your own understanding. In all your ways acknowledge him, and he will make your paths smooth.

Proverbs 3:5–6

Envision yourself deep in the Rockies. All is still and silent. Even the mischievous wind has bedded down for a rest along the narrow path. Not far ahead, a clearing appears amid the evergreens' deep shade. As you emerge, the setting sun reveals a stunning, nearly glowing landscape of white. A thick layer of pristine snow subtly glimmers across the mountain and from every bowing branch lining the slope. In the distance, snowcapped peaks pierce the orange and indigo sky. You move into the opening, and the fresh air nips at your cheeks and floods your body. In front of you, stillness extends, your path freer and smoother than flight.

Now imagine a hang glider launching off one of the rocky cliffs. Could you do that? Even if you couldn't physically do it, God invites you to hang glide spiritually, in a sense, by putting the full weight of your trust in Him as you take a step of faith. When we rely on our own strength, we confine ourselves to a lonely and aimless life, marked by uncertain and dangerous turns. When we acknowledge the Lord and His teachings, we glide on His strength and His resolve. These paths will take unexpected turns at times, but with Christ as our guide, we can confidently anticipate and travel the adventures ahead.

Tonight, consider the path before you. Perhaps you're contemplating a change the Lord is nudging you to make. Are you willing to "trust the Lord with all your heart"?

Racing to the Finish

Since we are surrounded by so many examples of faith, we must get rid of everything that slows us down, especially sin that distracts us. We must run the race that lies ahead of us and never give up. We must focus on Jesus, the source and goal of our faith.

Hebrews 12:1–2

The race stretches out before the runners, who stretch, jog in place, and talk to their companions. They have trained for this race, putting in long miles, lifting weights, visualizing the start, reviewing the course, and thinking about the joy of finishing. Persevering through the rainy days, the hot days, the snowy and cold days, the windy days, these athletes have not given up in pursuit of the finish line. Many have trained with friends, to spur them forward and help them focus on their ultimate goal: finishing the race.

The race to the finish begins long before the starting line. It began the day the individual decided to race. The training was part of the race, but everything culminates at the finish. All of their hard work, dedication, and planning is brought to completion with the crossing of the finish line.

Your spiritual journey is also a race with one ultimate goal: reaching the throne of God, with Jesus, your Lord and Savior, sitting next to Him. The apostle Paul urges you to be dedicated to reaching the goal, ignoring the pain and suffering of the race, throwing off the extra baggage of sin. Train diligently, acknowledging that your decision to train is the very start of the race. And keep in mind the "source and goal" of this race: Jesus.

This week, what will you do to be diligent about training?

Living a Sheltered Life

The eternal God is your shelter, and his everlasting arms support you. He will force your enemies out of your way and tell you to destroy them.

Deuteronomy 33:27

Shelter is one of the fundamental needs of human beings. Most of us think of our home as our shelter—a place where we feel safe and protected from harm, especially at night when the doors are locked and the shades drawn. Shelter comes in many forms—whether it's a tent for climbers in the Rockies, or a house on stilts in the Amazon River basin, an igloo, or even a mud hut. People around the globe create a shelter from the materials around them in order to live safe from the elements.

Today's passage contains some final words Moses spoke to the Israelites. Soon they would leave the wilderness for the Promised Land. Moses understood their fear of the future, of facing unknown enemies. He gave them a message of hope, assuring them of God's protection and provision as they sheltered in His everlasting arms.

Your feelings may mimic those of the Israelites when they faced an unknown future. The potential for tragedy or turmoil in other ways can seem ever present, affecting our ability to sleep. When you think about the future, what comes to mind? Fearful thoughts? Uncertainty? If so, consider the shelter Moses discovered. Like the Israelites, you can relax in the shelter of God's everlasting arms and trust your future to Him.

Strength to Endure

My brothers and sisters, be very happy when you are tested in different ways. You know that such testing of your faith produces endurance. Endure until your testing is over. Then you will be mature and complete.

James 1:2–4

Bristlecone pine trees, found mainly in California, are the oldest trees on earth. In fact, there is one tree in particular, Methuselah, named after the oldest man in the Bible. Scientists bored a small hole in its trunk to count the rings and found the tree to be over 4,700 years old.

In looking at the rings, scientists were also able to discover in what years droughts occurred, when there was ample rainfall, and when swarms of insect pests caused damage. The tree had been through quite a bit in its life span of almost five millennia. Yet it endured and continued to grow in both drought and plenty.

While the apostle James might not have known about bristlecone pines, he knew quite a bit about living the Christian life. In his letter to fellow Christians, he reminds us that troublesome times can lead to growth.

Endurance makes you stronger. When your faith is tested, you'll find out exactly where your strength originates. And once you figure out that Jesus provides every ounce of strength you'll ever need, Christian maturity is developed. You'll never stop learning and growing, but you'll no longer need reassurance that Jesus is with you—you just know it for certain.

So look at those times of drought and pestilence as a chance to learn and grow deeper in your walk with Jesus. Find joy as you grow.

Inspiration

But no one asks, "Where is God, my Creator, who inspires songs in the night, who teaches us more than he teaches the animals of the earth, who makes us wiser than the birds in the sky?"

Job 35:10–11

It's bedtime. You should be sleepy, but you're just not able to relax. Your brain's busy mulling over tomorrow's to-do list, and you can't settle down. So what puts you in a restful mood? Reading a chapter or two? Listening to your favorite CDs? What is your music of choice? Country music? Pop? Gospel? Classical?

Elihu, a friend of Job, suggested another type of music—songs inspired by God. While the Bible is not specific on the types of songs imagined by Elihu, we can't help thinking of the songs of the Bible: the Psalms.

Tucked under the covers, reading a bedtime devotional that describes God's ability to "inspire songs in the night," perhaps you're wondering, Can God really do that for me, even if I'm struggling financially? Having problems with my boss? Coping with my mother's serious health issues?

Your life does not have to be 100 percent perfect before God can give you a song in the night. If you look back at the Psalms, you will see that life wasn't at all rosy for many psalmists. Yet they acknowledged that God was still good, even when life was at its worst. Turn your thoughts toward God. Revel in His presence, His love, His care. Hum a favorite hymn. And fall to sleep.

Tit for Tat

So place yourselves under God's authority. Resist the devil,
and he will run away from you. Come close to God, and he
will come close to you.

James 4:7–8

Quid pro quo. It's a Latin phrase meaning an equal exchange or
"tit for tat." You often hear implied quid pro quo. "When you
empty the dishwasher, I will drive you to the mall to get some
shoes," is something a parent might say to her teenager. When
you're at church and a woman comes to you saying, "I want to
give you a big hug," there's an inner reciprocal urge and quickly
you both embrace.

To the Christian, this Latin phrase suggests that when you
come closer to God, He will move equally closer to you. Of course,
you can never out-give our wise, powerful God, but this verse
shows that everyone has an obligation in the maintenance of this
holy relationship. God will not force Himself upon you; it can't be
a one-sided connection. You must show desire and initiative. As
you draw close to God, you become a magnet that attracts God.

A mother loves to hold and snuggle her precious child. No
mom would have her daughter come with those outstretched arms
pleading, "Hold me," and then snub her. As God's little girl, when
you come to Him you get open arms . . . every time. Some days,
you may even feel like crawling up in His lap and staying. Isn't
it comforting to be in His magnificent presence and authority?
And when you're in God's lap, the devil will run away from you.

I Cannot Be Moved

I will praise the LORD, who advises me. My conscience warns me at night. I always keep the LORD in front of me. When he is by my side, I cannot be moved.

Psalm 16:7–8

The words "I cannot be moved" from the Scripture might seem familiar because they are used in the hymn "I Shall Not Be Moved." Many children are taught this song. However, in a child's understanding, the meaning behind the lyrics must seem obscure. What kind of spiritual significance is found in the words "I shall not be moved"?

The words are full of determination—the will, the resolve, the intent to stay put. In Psalm 16, David, who had the reputation of being a man after God's own heart (1 Samuel 13:14), explained his resolve to cling to God. Instead of trusting in his weapons or his soldiers, he placed the full weight of his trust in God's protection, knowing that nothing could move him with an immovable God at his side. Centuries later, Jesus would encourage His followers to do the same (John 15:4–8).

He wants that same "I cannot be moved" response from you. His constant availability gives you the opportunity to communicate with Him all day every day—and all night as well! He offers you advice through His Word and His Spirit. He's ready to respond to your questions, your prayers, and your concerns anytime.

As you tuck the covers under your chin, remind yourself of David's assurance, "Complete joy is in your presence. Pleasures are by your side forever" (Psalm 16:11).

Beacon of Light

*So we regard the words of the prophets as confirmed beyond
all doubt. You're doing well by paying attention to their words.
Continue to pay attention as you would to a light that shines
in a dark place as you wait for day to come and the morning
star to rise in your hearts.*

2 Peter 1:19

Have you ever been at a low point in your life and found yourself
wallowing in a dark, hopeless place? Perhaps in the mire you cried
out for God to lift you out of it. Maybe it happened instantly or
it took months. Maybe words of comfort were whispered to you
by the Holy Spirit, or you heard them from a friend, or gleaned
them from a Bible verse. Whatever the source, this word of encouragement and hope pierced the dark and shed a ray of light
in your heart.

As the apostle Peter explains, God's prophets foretold the
blessed arrival of the Word made flesh, imparting hope to God's
people in the dark and sometimes hopeless days of old. But their
words are also directed toward modern, twenty-first century you,
as a reminder that Jesus' light will shine brightly again in your
heart. Isaiah 45:3 promises, "I will give you treasures from dark
places and hidden stockpiles. Then you will know that I, the Lord
God of Israel, have called you by name." Be encouraged! Even in
the hardest and darkest of times, there are treasures just waiting
to be revealed to you, who are cherished and called by name.

Place the words of the prophets into your modern context and
you'll find they are indeed a timeless beacon of truth designed
long ago, which pave the way for the morning star to rise in and
lift your heart.

Load Carrier

Turn your burdens over to the LORD, and he will take care of you. He will never let the righteous person stumble.

Psalm 55:22

Before the invention of cars and trucks and trains, explorers and traders often used horses, donkeys, and mules as pack animals to carry their equipment and goods across unknown territory. Traditional pack animals in other regions of the world include llamas, Bactrian camels, dromedary camels, yaks, elephants, water buffalos, dogs, and reindeer. Every animal carries its load on its back in some style of backpack.

Let's be honest. You probably don't associate with pack-carrying beasts of burden in your daily schedule. But perhaps you're a burden-bearer yourself—burdens of the emotional kind. David, one of the ancient kings of Israel, knew all about burdens.

When David wrote Psalm 55, he was dealing with the burden of betrayal, having been double-crossed by someone he trusted. In his suffering, David recognized the One who could help him carry his burden of anguish, grief, and despair—his Lord. Consequently, he encouraged all to "turn your burdens over to the Lord."

What are your burdens? If you're carrying around a purse full of painful burdens tonight (and even a stylish purse doesn't make the burden any lighter), know that you don't have to bear the weight alone. The Lord is ever present and ready to assist you and take care of you. As you pray, take time to name each one. Let Him lighten your load.

Misty Morning

Then your light will break through like the dawn, and you will heal quickly. Your righteousness will go ahead of you, and the glory of the LORD will guard you from behind.

Isaiah 58:8

In the northern portions of the United States, usually during the spring and fall, many early mornings are dark and gray, shrouded in dense fog. Folks who live in those regions know that in only a matter of hours the mist will burn off, allowing the sun to break through.

Knowing that the sun is coming certainly brings joy. But in the midst of the cold, damp fog, where you can't see ten feet in front of you, you might wonder if the sun will shine at all. Sometimes the fog isn't outside, but inside. Things just aren't going well and it's hard to see—even harder to believe—that the sun will ever warm you again.

Isaiah knew what it was like to wonder when the sun would shine again. The people to whom he prophesied were not obeying the Lord and something akin to darkness and fog shrouded the nation. The people needed to return to the Lord and follow Him. If they would do so, His light would break through and bring healing.

If you're in a fog today, desperately waiting for the mist to lift and the sun to break through, take God's hand and talk to Him. Ask Him to show you anything in your life that needs His light to shine in, to heal, to cleanse. When you do that, the mist will clear and the "light will break through like the dawn."

Moonstruck

Like the moon his throne will stand firm forever. It will be like a faithful witness in heaven.

Psalm 89:37

When you step outside into a dark, clear night, there's a chance you'll look up at the stars and scan the sky, searching for the moon. A full moon engulfs you with its powerful magnetism, its beauty, its promise of romance.

The phases of the moon remain as predictable now as they were thousands of years ago. That's why the moon was the perfect metaphor for King David's dynasty. After rejecting David's offer to build a temple, God made a covenant with David concerning his descendants (2 Samuel 7:11–16). Not only would David's son ascend the throne, but centuries later, a Messiah would come from David's family line. This Messiah—Jesus—will be King forever.

This passage also is a tribute to God's faithfulness in bringing about His promises. His love and faithfulness work together. He doesn't spoon out His love one bite at a time nor does He measure your love for Him and match His love to that equation. Instead, He freely offers the full measure of His love to each person.

Are you unsure about God's love for you? You can fix that tonight before you fall to sleep. Close your eyes and call His name. Confess any doubts you might have. Then cling to Him, for He promises to respond when He hears your call. Like the moon, His throne will stand firm forever.

Every Day without Fail

*When Daniel learned that the document had been signed,
he went to his house. . . . Three times each day he got down
on his knees and prayed to his God. He had always praised
God this way.*

Daniel 6:10

What do you do every day without fail? Chances are you at least
brush your teeth and put on some makeup. Maybe you also have
to walk the dog or hit the gym for your daily exercise.

What about prayer? Do you do that every day, without fail?

Daniel did. He prayed three times a day; in fact, the verse
says "He had always praised God this way." But it wasn't an
easy situation. Daniel was in Babylon, the land where he had
been taken captive when the Babylonians destroyed his nation.
He had risen to a position of trust and power with the king. But
at one point, the Babylonian king issued an edict that for thirty
days, everyone in the kingdom must pray only to him.

When this occurred, what did Daniel do? He went to his room,
opened the windows, "got down on his knees and prayed to his
God." Not to the king. Darius was just a man. Why pray to someone who couldn't read his thoughts, know his heart, or answer his
prayers? Why desert the God who had seen him through so much
in his life just to save his job for the next thirty days?

Daniel's unwavering faith provides an example of how you
should never lose hope, even in the worst of circumstances. God
will reward your faithfulness to Him.

So, along with the rest of your daily routine this morning,
take a moment to pray.

Seeking the Light

Your word is a lamp for my feet and a light for my path.
Psalm 119:105

What is your favorite source when you need directions? The GPS in your car or phone? MapQuest? The atlas tucked under the seat of your car? Your grandfather's compass? The more trusted the source, the better.

The writer of Psalm 119 invites you to consider a source of direction that many trust. Psalm 119, the longest psalm in the Bible, catalogues the ways that God's Word—His laws and decrees—directs our paths.

Consider the stories in the Bible of people exposed to the light of God literally and figuratively. God appeared as a pillar of fire to guide the people of Israel to the Promised Land (Exodus 13:21–22). Jesus described Himself as the "light of the world" (John 8:12). Saul of Tarsus experienced a dramatic encounter with the "light of the world" on the road to Damascus (Acts 9). God appeared as a burning bush to Moses (Exodus 3). But Psalm 119:105 refers to God's light as God's revelation—His revealing of who He is and how He works through His creation.

Perhaps tonight you're in need of illumination in the midst of a confusing situation. Open God's Word. It is a lamp for your feet and a light for your path, allowing you to walk carefully without fear of falling. Know that even when you turn out the light to sleep, you can rest in the promise of God's light.

The Morning News

The righteous LORD is in that city. He does no wrong. He brings his judgment to light every morning. He does not fail.

Zephaniah 3:5

Sometimes it can be difficult to set foot into a new day. The world can be a difficult, wearying place (just read the morning paper) and we wonder what difference our little steps of obedience can possibly make.

Zephaniah was a prophet to Judah (the southern kingdom of Israel) shortly before its destruction. He tried to call the people back to God for they had become complacent, refusing correction, caring for no one (3:1–4). King Josiah was willing to follow the prophet's direction and instituted reforms in an attempt to bring the people back to God. Unfortunately, most of the people continued in their sinful ways.

Yet verse 5 brings a ray of hope: Even though the city was filled with sin, "the righteous Lord is in that city." His holiness was not affected by His surroundings. And He consistently brought justice. No matter how things looked in the world, God Himself will never fail.

The world today is no different from Zephaniah's world. Sin still exists, pain occurs, people are hurting. God is no different either. He is still holy. His justice is still a beacon of light. He will never fail.

So step into your day with the knowledge that you're on the winning side. Your God will never fail. God needs people like you to go out there and do His will in your little corner of the world.

From God's Hand

What do people get from all of their hard work and struggles under the sun? Their entire life is filled with pain, and their work is unbearable. Even at night their minds don't rest. Even this is pointless.

Ecclesiastes 2:22–23

Some might ask themselves, "Why did I bother?" when a frustrating outcome is the result of hours or years of hard effort. For example, when you spent hours cleaning the house for a family gathering only to find your efforts criticized or undermined by others trashing the house. Or, if you spent years chasing after a dream only to have the dream become a nightmare. This realization sadly turns to bitterness or disillusionment.

Perhaps you're feeling like that right now. The writer of Ecclesiastes isn't telling you to adopt a "why bother" attitude, even though he alludes to some activities as pointless. Worrying about matters totally outside the realm of your control or spending your whole life chasing after satisfaction outside of the will of God is like trying to sweep the sand off the beach—pointless. But just one verse later, he leads us to the right attitude: "There is nothing better for people to do than to eat, drink, and find satisfaction in their work. I saw that even this comes from the hand of God" (Ecclesiastes 2:24). Note that satisfaction comes "from the hand of God."

You have access to a heavenly Father who craves your friendship and obedience to His ways. In return, He allows joy and peace to saturate your spirit. Turn your mind to Him as you settle into bed this evening. Allow yourself to be comforted by His Spirit. Smile. Now slide into your night of sleep.

Light Shine

*Light exposes the true character of everything because light
makes everything easy to see. That's why it says: "Wake up,
sleeper! Rise from the dead, and Christ will shine on you."*

Ephesians 5:13–14

If you've ever gone camping—really roughing it with a tent in the
middle of the woods—you know how dark the night can really be.
Every little noise is magnified in the inky blackness, making you
wonder what animals are in the woods and how close they are.

In the daylight when you pitched your tent, it seemed to be
the perfect spot. The only reason it's scary now is that, when you
unzip the tent flap, you can't see a thing!

Physical darkness can be frightening. But even more dread-
ful is spiritual darkness—the place where evil intentions thrive.
Before you gave your heart to Christ, your soul was in spiritual
darkness, dead to the goodness of God. When you answered the
gentle nudging of the Holy Spirit and received the gift of salvation, your soul "woke up." The light of Christ surrounded you,
shining brightly upon the evil that once held you captive, driving
it all away.

As a Christian, God's light illuminates your life. Those who
are lost will see Christ's light in you and be drawn to it. When
others ask you the source of your light, are you always ready
"to defend your confidence in God when anyone asks you to
explain it" (1 Peter 3:15)? There is no greater joy than telling
someone about the gift of salvation and seeing his or her eyes
light up with new life.

Ask the Lord to let you help your light shine today.

Counting Sheep

Let godly people triumph in glory. Let them sing for joy on their beds.

Psalm 149:5

The search for a good night's sleep began long ago. Ancient Persians improved the quality of their sleep by using goatskins filled with water to make beds. The Romans stuffed cloth bags with wool, hay, or reeds—the wealthy preferred feather stuffing. In the sixteenth century, people built timber bed frames to hold their mattresses. The invention of the innerspring mattress in 1871 by Heinrich Westphal led to softer, more comfortable beds.

Today mattress companies promise in their ads that their pillow-top mattresses, adjustable mattresses, or waterbeds will provide restful sleep. However, even if you sleep on a mattress that's built using the highest level of technology, you might still have nights when you're counting sheep in order to sleep. Sometimes the worries and frustrations of the day keep sleep at bay.

The first sentence of today's Scripture verse challenges you to approach sleep with a right attitude toward God. Recognizing His authority over all creatures and all creation as well as yourself and every aspect of your life can release you from that heaviness that interrupts your sleep. Do that and you will be able to follow the verse's presleep pattern: Sing for joy on your bed. Thank God through songs of praise. Believe He is able to fill you with contentment and rest as you praise His name.

And you won't need to count sheep!

Spiritual Fitness

Is anything too hard for the LORD?
Genesis 18:14

Why is it that getting into shape takes months of disciplined exercise, but getting out of shape is so incredibly easy? We wake every morning full of resolve that this will be the day, the month, the year that we finally drop those extra pounds or run that 5K race. But life pulls us in dozens of different directions, and often it seems just too plain difficult to keep those well-intended resolutions.

Lots of things in life can be tough, like maintaining muscle mass. Scripture tells us, however, that nothing is too hard for God. In Genesis we read the amazing account of God's promise to Abraham and Sarah that they will have a child in their old age. Now what kind of shape does an elderly woman need to be in for that to happen?

If God could quicken the womb of a woman in her nineties, He can work in your situation today as well. His ability to intervene has nothing to do with how "fit" you appear to be. First Corinthians 1:27 describes how much God delights in using the weak to accomplish His purposes: "God chose what the world considers nonsense to put wise people to shame. God chose what the world considers weak to put what is strong to shame."

Lace up those exercise shoes and head out this morning with a smile on your face.

Nothing is too difficult for God.

The Oasis

Forget what happened in the past, and do not dwell on events from long ago. I am going to do something new. It is already happening. Don't you recognize it? I will clear a way in the desert. I will make rivers on dry land.

Isaiah 43:18–19

It's not fun to remember "living in the desert" experiences—times of overpowering problems with undetermined solutions. Desert living makes your thirst for life evaporate as you analyze your choices for the future. It causes you to imagine a tomorrow that mimics past miserable situations with no guarantees of a better future.

The book of Isaiah gives some helpful advice straight out of the mouth of God. "Forget what happened in the past," says the Lord. But how can I forget about the past? you might ask yourself. Those times of severe thirst and dryness have left indelible marks. I can't shake off the memories.

You can stop focusing on the past and look to the future because of God's promise: "I am going to do something new. It is already happening." Take a look around you and purposefully search for signs of God's hand at work in your life. Remember how He answered past prayers to meet your specific needs. Dwell on how faithful He has been to uphold and guide you through previous difficult situations.

The God who, like an oasis, can "make rivers on dry land" promises to refresh you, encourage you, and enable you to live a life pleasing to Him. Walk into the cool water of His love and relax into a deep sleep tonight.

Molded into His Image

I encourage you to offer your bodies as living sacrifices, dedicated to God and pleasing to him. . . . Don't become like the people of this world. Instead, change the way you think. Then you will always be able to determine what God really wants—what is good, pleasing, and perfect.

Romans 12:1–2

The world in which you live shapes you, and often the molding is slow and subtle. The way you think about the world is affected by your family, your friends, and your co-workers. How often, however, is it shaped by the words of Christ?

Paul encouraged us to think of ourselves as living sacrifices, dedicated to God and pleasing to Him. We are not to be like the people of this world but to change the way we think. But how do we do that?

You can begin by thinking about what you think about. Consider which of your ideas, values, and opinions have been shaped by the world and which have been truly shaped by the Word of God. Examine the development of your opinions and you will see the development of your maturity; then consider any subtle influence from popular culture. This will show you which ways of thinking need to be changed in order to conform with Christ's way of thinking and which should be honed and strengthened to His glory.

Search every part of your life and you may find a rogue thought that needs to be submitted to the control of the Father. Rejoice that your Father holds you to a high standard and is pleased to give you the strength and wisdom to strive to reach it. Ask Him today to mold and shape you into what He wants you to be.

Heroes

*The LORD your God is with you. He is a hero who saves you.
He happily rejoices over you, renews you with his love, and
celebrates over you with shouts of joy.*

Zephaniah 3:17

History is loaded with heroes and heroines. Florence Nightingale
was honored for revolutionizing nursing care during the Crimean
War. Rosa Parks was respected for refusing to sit at the back of
the bus at the beginnings of the Civil Rights movement, and
Marie Curie admired for the discovery of radium and polonium.
Or maybe your hero is that nurse at the ER who stayed with you
through a difficult time.

Heroes often reflect similar traits: courage, determination, a
desire for justice. That's why children love to pretend to be heroes.
One compound word, however, sums up a hero's mandatory trait:
self-sacrifice. They often face health problems, incarceration,
life-threatening situations, or death for their causes.

How does God fit into the above description of heroes? That's
easy. He gave His Son Jesus to save you from your sins. Jesus'
sacrifice opened the door to God's love and makes a personal
relationship with Him possible.

God rejoices when you accept His love, when you listen to
His Spirit, when you talk to Him in prayer. As you prepare to
sleep, allow your mind to dwell on the marvelous result of God's
sacrifice—your relationship with Him. Ask Him to use that relationship to share His truth with the world. When you follow
God's example of self-sacrifice, you will be a hero.

He Hears You

We are confident that God listens to us if we ask for anything that has his approval. We know that he listens to our requests. So we know that we already have what we ask him for.

1 John 5:14–15

What does it mean that whatever we request "we already have what we ask for"? How can God make such a promise? Often we wonder if He's really going to give us the answer we desire.

The key is found in your relationship with Him. For example, if one of your children asks you if she can play in the street, you say no. She may not understand that because she sees that the street is a perfect location for roller blading. But you know the dangers of playing in the street and wisely tell her no. It's much the same with prayer. While many of your requests make perfect sense to you, God wisely says no at times because He sees the bigger picture.

But what about those prayers that you assume would have God's approval—the healing of a sick person, the salvation of a family member, the protection of a loved one? How do you understand His no in those situations? Again, the key is found in your relationship with Him. Do you trust Him enough to let Him do what He knows is best? Do you realize that, in His great love for you, He will always do what is good even when you can't see it?

The promise to take to heart this morning is that God listens. You "can go confidently to the throne of God's kindness to receive mercy and find kindness" (Hebrews 4:16). God always hears you and He promises to answer.

The Peace Prize

I've told you this so that my peace will be with you. In the world you'll have trouble. But cheer up! I have overcome the world.

John 16:33

Everybody enjoys wining a prize, even if the prize is not expensive. For example, the door prize at a meeting, the blue ribbon for the best flower in the garden show, or the clever gadget at the kitchenware party. Winning a prize brings a smile to your face and a jolt of excitement to your brain. However, there's one kind of prize that your hands don't hold. It's the peace that Jesus gives to those who love Him.

When Jesus says, "My peace will be with you," He's not promising you a trouble-free life. He's talking about providing you with peace of mind and heart. By trusting Jesus enough to turn your life over to Him and agreeing to follow His leading in your everyday activities, you open the door to His peace gift. Having His peace doesn't mean you'll quickly find the answers to all your problems. Instead, you'll have the assurance that Jesus is bigger than those problems and that He will help you find solutions because He proclaimed, "I have overcome the world."

This peace prize is available to you tonight. If fears or worries threaten your sleep, remember the peace Jesus offers. Close your eyes, and place your complete confidence in Him. Allow His peace to blanket you and go to sleep.

Taking the First Step

*Early the next morning Abraham saddled his donkey. He took
with him two of his servants and his son Isaac. When he had
cut the wood for the burnt offering, he set out for the place that
God had told him about.*

Genesis 22:3

What was your first conscious thought when you woke up this
morning? Did you think, "Great! Another day! I can't wait to get
up and get going"? Or, did your mind instantly begin to mull over
the potential problems that today presents? Maybe you're facing
a difficult situation at work, or you have a medical concern that
defies diagnosis. Perhaps guests are due to arrive and you don't
feel prepared, or there's simply too much to do and too little of
you to go around. The bridge you have to cross from the start to
the completion of today's tasks looks a mile long.

God gave Abraham a difficult assignment—the hardest in the
world. Abraham was to sacrifice his son—the child of promise.
This was not the despicable command of a divine despot but rather
a tough test administered by a tender Teacher.

How could Abraham bring himself to face the day on which
he was to sacrifice his son? We aren't given many details, but
knowing what lay ahead that day must have made starting it full
of anxiety. Yet Abraham saddled the donkey, cut the wood, and
headed into history. But a good outcome awaited.

Do you have any bridges you think you will be unable to cross
today? Just focus on what needs to be done right now. Saddle up,
cut the wood, and set out into your day. Take the first step. And
trust God to take the rest.

Every Thought

We take every thought captive so that it is obedient to Christ.
2 Corinthians 10:5

In this media-controlled world, it's easy to let your thoughts be dominated by what's going on around you. Newspaper and internet headlines and sound bites describe catastrophes in bold-faced type. Magazine covers display scantily clothed models wearing the latest styles. Your car radio keeps you updated on the latest accidents, crimes, and violence surrounding your community. Television programs portray dysfunctional families living immoral lives. Sometimes we feel overwhelmed by the turmoil or dysfunction around us.

As you prepare for bed with your mind filtering the day's debris, how can you possibly "take every thought captive so that it is obedient to Christ" as the apostle Paul suggests? Keep in mind that Paul traveled through many cities and towns where a licentious lifestyle was the norm. So, he knew the discipline of corralling stray thoughts. It can be as difficult as herding cats.

Philippians 4:8 identifies a way of thinking that you can cultivate before you sleep: "Keep your thoughts on whatever is right or deserves praise: things that are true, honorable, fair, pure, acceptable, or commendable."

When you lie down to sleep tonight, turn your mind to the good things you have in Christ. Note the many times when God has supplied your needs. Think of the power He gives you to be obedient to His directions, then go to sleep.

Family Tree

Keep in mind that the LORD your God is the only God. He is a faithful God, who keeps his promise and is merciful to thousands of generations of those who love him and obey his commands.

Deuteronomy 7:9

Have you shinnied up your family tree lately? Establishing kinship with distant ancestors can be a highly complicated process involving historical research and sometimes sophisticated genetic analysis as well. Google the single word "genealogy" on the internet and you'll come up with over 91 million entries.

It's only natural to wonder about those we've descended from, but time can be devoted more productively to the generations that will follow our own. How can you be sure that you're investing wisely in your human family?

As the people of Israel waited to enter the Promised Land, Moses reminded them of the faithful God who brought them there. He wanted them to invest in a legacy of obedience to the one and only God. He also reminded them of their genealogy as the people of God, for He chose them and promised to always be faithful to them. They had only to consider the past—how God led them out of slavery in Egypt—to see that God kept His promises.

We serve a God who is absolutely faithful to His people and promises to be merciful to "thousands of generations" of those who obey Him. That's why the most important investment you can make in the lives of your descendants is to love God and live by His commands. A spiritual investment now will reap divine dividends in the future. How will you add to that investment today?

Heavenly Comforter

Praise the God and Father of our Lord Jesus Christ! . . . He comforts us whenever we suffer. That is why whenever other people suffer, we are able to comfort them by using the same comfort we have received from God.

2 Corinthians 1:3–4

It has been said that unless you experience a lack of some kind, you can't know God as Provider. Unless you experience pain and illness, you can't know God as Healer. And unless you experience suffering, you can't know God as Comforter. Through every kind of trouble that you meet along your path, God will reveal another aspect of Himself to you in a very personal way if you're looking.

What are you suffering from? Has grief over a loss overtaken you? Has depression wound its way through your life so as to choke any hope of joy out of it? Has a financial situation dumped an insurmountable load on your shoulders?

Tonight, as you escape from a cold world into the temporary protection of your cozy, warm bed, consider the ways that the Lord has comforted you during periods of suffering. Perhaps He consoled you through the timely encouragement of a friend. Maybe He opened your eyes to see new meaning in a familiar verse of Scripture. Or maybe He painted an otherworldly evening landscape as the sun slipped below a rose-colored horizon—just for you.

A compassionate God bestows comfort on His beloved in tangible ways. He wants you comforted so you can, in turn, comfort someone else. And in so doing, you deepen your relationship with your heavenly Father. What can be more comforting than that?

Seeing the Son

Light is sweet, and it is good for one's eyes to see the sun.

Ecclesiastes 11:7

It hasn't been clearly identified until recent years, but thousands of people know what it's like to experience the aptly named S.A.D., Seasonal Affective Disorder. This condition can cause lethargy, mental fatigue, and feelings of depression due to insufficient exposure to natural light. Scientists and physicians have affirmed the importance of sunlight to the human body—a physiological fact that Scripture has acknowledged all along.

While not everyone experiences S.A.D., it's true that most of us feel more cheerful when the sun is shining. Sunlight affects our mood in multiple ways. It not only provides illumination for our daily activities but also essential amounts of Vitamin D.

Exposure to God's Word is also vital to well-being. Think of it as "Vitamin D for the soul." When you begin your day with prayer and Scripture reading and take a few moments to meditate on biblical principles, you can be assured that the rest of your day will bear a marked difference. You might awake under a personal dark cloud, but looking into the light of God's Word provides a critical "perspective corrective."

Just as it is "good for one's eyes to see the sun," so also it is good for the soul to see the image of the Son of God in the pages of His Word.

Priorities

Keep your mind on things above, not on worldly things.

Colossians 3:2

The house rests. The TV is turned off and nightly rituals commence as you head for bed. You pass by sleeping children, taking a quick peek into their rooms. Or you pass images in silver frames of the children in your life who are important to you.

What about the futures of those special children? You may often wonder if they will make good grades, attend college, be popular, excel in sports, or find the right person to marry or the right career to follow. While you cheer along with them any successes they have in life, you also want to somehow show them that those types of successes are never more important than knowing Jesus.

Before you sleep tonight, pray for the children in your world—whether your own, your nieces and nephews, or other children you care about. Ask God to touch their lives and to teach them His ways. Ask that He help them keep their minds on things above, as the apostle Paul advised in his letter to the Colossians. Pray that their attitudes and actions will reflect God and that He will help them stand strong and reject the world's priorities.

And then take a few minutes to think about this for your own life. In what ways are you (or are you not) keeping your mind on things above and not on worldly things? How are your personal priorities shaping up?

After the Rain

*I am confident and unafraid, because the LORD is my strength
and my song. He is my Savior. With joy you will draw water
from the springs of salvation.*

Isaiah 12:2–3

When the sun comes out after a rainstorm, the sunshine seems
brighter, doesn't it? And with the sky washed by rain, it never
looks bluer. As the sun comes out on the newly washed world,
you feel a discernible lift to your spirits. The same is true when a
relationship is mended after a stormy time of misunderstandings
and other emotional pain. Although dear before, the relationship
seems all the more precious.

The Old Testament prophet Isaiah described the relief and joy
the nation of Israel would feel once they regained the Lord's favor.
After years of disobedience, they would suffer the consequences
of their behavior when their enemies conquered them and carried
them off into a foreign land. But just as He delivered His people
from slavery in Egypt centuries before, God would rescue His
people after their time of exile. The sunshine of His love would
roll away the clouds of oppression and lift their spirits.

Perhaps today, you're wondering if you'll ever get to the
"after" phase of a broken relationship. Perhaps that broken relationship is with God and you wonder if you'll ever again have
His favor. If so, let this passage in Isaiah be a reminder of God's
willingness to comfort you. He simply waits for you to take the
first step toward Him. You can go to Him "confident and unafraid"
that He will listen.

True Security

Don't love money. Be happy with what you have because God has said, "I will never abandon you or leave you."

Hebrews 13:5

You've seen them. Dogs or cats rifling through the trash cans or wandering aimlessly down the street or across your back fence, abandoned by their owners. Animals aren't the only creatures or things that people desert. Many communities have their back streets of abandoned houses, unfinished buildings, and property crammed with broken-down vehicles. Their streets may hold abandoned people, too—the homeless, the helpless, the down-and-outers. The face of abandonment isn't pretty.

Perhaps it's the fear of abandonment that causes people to place money at the top of their "want" list. The story goes that someone asked a rich man, "How much more money do you need to be satisfied?" only to have him reply, "Just a little bit more." Trying to make enough money to be satisfied is an exercise in futility because you'll always want more. Since having money doesn't guarantee contentment, the writer of Hebrews admonishes us to be happy with what we have.

So how can you sleep tonight without worrying about tomorrow? You can be secure in God's presence. You will never be abandoned. When you worship Him with your heart, soul, mind, and strength (Matthew 22:37), you'll find yourself assured and confident of His presence and care. That's much more precious than money.

Be Our Strength

O Lord, have pity on us. We wait with hope for you. Be our strength in the morning. Yes, be our savior in times of trouble.

Isaiah 33:2

If you're a morning person, perhaps you feel especially energized as the morning light peeks through the window, signaling the dawn of a new day. You feel like leaping out of bed as early as possible, ready to sing, right? Not always! Even a morning person has a hard time getting up when a difficult day dawns.

Days like that feel like barbells with extra weights attached. As you progress through the day, it's as if extra weights have been added to each side—weights beyond your capacity to lift cleanly. As a result, you feel as if you'll be crushed beneath the weight.

Is today that kind of day? Consider the words of the prophet Isaiah. Still predicting a time of future turmoil for Israel, Isaiah prophesied their anguish. But they wouldn't simply despair. Instead, they would call upon the Lord—the only one who could lift the weight of their despair.

Like the people of Israel, you're invited to cry out to the Lord. Ask Him to be your strength this morning. Remember: he doesn't just want to be a spotter—the person who watches you lift weights safely. He wants to be the ultimate weight lifter in your life. Give Him the problems that weigh you down, then sit back and watch Him lift them.

A Rest That Refreshes

I will give those who are weary all they need. I will refresh everyone who is filled with sorrow.

Jeremiah 31:25

Let's face it. At the end of some days you're completely wiped out. Any combination of negative experiences can make you feel that way. Perhaps your car stalled in the middle of a busy intersection, people squabbled about insignificant issues at your workplace, or you've just learned someone you love has cancer. Your mind and spirit beg to be refreshed. If so, this verse from Jeremiah has a promise you can take to heart: "I will refresh everyone who is filled with sorrow." That promise doesn't have a cancellation clause, or a "good until" date. Just as God promised to restore the Israelites after they were broken in exile, He's always ready to renew and refresh your hope.

In need of renewal? God often works through people and circumstances to accomplish His desires. Reread Jeremiah 31:25, saying the words quietly out loud as a way of owning this promise. Then play one of your favorite worship songs. Remember a specific instance of God's goodness. Bask in His love as you pray for Him to bring refreshment in your life—a balm as welcome as a soft hammock on a desert island. Put your day behind you, and absorb the hope that God offers when you lean on Him. Let your hope in Him cover you as you fall asleep.

Strong Support

*Don't be afraid, because I am with you. Don't be intimidated;
I am your God. I will strengthen you. I will help you. I will
support you with my victorious right hand.*

Isaiah 41:10

Gothic cathedrals overwhelm us with their beauty—the cavernous
interior spaces with crypts and stained-glass windows and ceilings
seemingly miles above still create awe for visitors who silently
bow in worship or crane their necks in an attempt to take it all in.

The reason these huge cathedrals can stand with seemingly
little support from within is because of projecting masonry structures that support the weight of the roof from the outside. These
structures are called "buttresses." On most medieval cathedrals,
these were designed as half-arches coming out from the roof to
the ground below. These "flying buttresses" played a huge part
in allowing the architects of these ancient buildings to create vast
open inner spaces for worship. And the fact that these cathedrals
are still standing—many of them surviving through two World
Wars—is a testament to the strength of these supports.

The prophet Isaiah mentions a different type of buttress—one
for the soul. The Creator of the universe offers the support of
His "victorious right hand." With the promise of His support
and strength, can't you just feel your soul enlarge? As with the
cathedrals, this creates more space within us for worship. Best
of all, this support isn't temporary—it's eternal.

In the midst of a tough time? God has you in the palm of His
strong right hand. He's willing to trade His strength for your fears.

The Ride of Your Life

The one who is testifying to these things says, "Yes, I'm coming soon!" Amen! Come, Lord Jesus! The good will of the Lord Jesus be with all of you. Amen!

Revelation 22:20–21

If you've ever enjoyed the entertainment of a late summer county fair, you well remember the cotton candy, the carnival games, and the midway—the merry-go-round with its colorful horses, the floating swings, and the sure-to-make-you-sick spinning cars, all culminating in the spectacular Ferris wheel. From the top, you could see the entire fairgrounds, partway around you could yell down to your friends and wave frantically.

But first, you always had to wait in line—sometimes what seemed like an endless line. You counted the times around, you waved to your friends, and you inched forward until you were finally locked in place in your own seat. And then, up you went!

Perhaps you're feeling restless now as you seem to be waiting in an endless line for your heavenly Father to fill you in on what your future holds. You're wondering when He will return and what that will really be like. Take heart. The Lord promises that He will be coming soon, and at just the perfect time.

As you close your eyes tonight, envision your Lord taking you on the ride of your life—for the rest of your time here and on into eternity. Like the Ferris wheel, riding with the Lord will surprise you with a high-flying feeling of excitement. And that ride begins this moment, as you close your eyes and yield to His will and His timing.

Aging Gratefully

Even when you're old, I'll take care of you. Even when your hair turns gray, I'll support you. I made you and will continue to care for you. I'll support you and save you.

Isaiah 46:4

Have you ever looked in the mirror first thing in the morning and wondered at the stranger staring back at you? Where did those stray gray hairs come from or the little lines radiating from your eyes? Why is it harder than ever to keep your weight under control? Even if you're not quite at the gray hair stage, maybe you feel older due to changes and challenges in your life now.

The months and years revolve so quickly that our external features show signs of age even while we feel no differently inside than we did when we were in high school. Nothing in our world seems constant except for change.

But there is something we can count on, however: the love and support of our heavenly Father. The years you've clocked on your personal odometer are incidental to Him. "Even when you're old," He reassures us in Isaiah, "I'll take care of you."

Do you sometimes fear the aging process? Wondering about the future can indeed be unnerving. Hear the words of your loving Lord: "I made you and will continue to care for you." So look in the mirror with new eyes—His eyes. Then resolve to celebrate this season of your life.

The Right Time

We can go confidently to the throne of God's kindness to receive mercy and find kindness, which will help us at the right time.

Hebrews 4:16

You're familiar with the scene—a long trip in a cramped car occupied by you, maybe another adult, and at least one child. The trees and buildings speed by, but even though you're making great time, the inevitable question resonates from the backseat: "Are we there yet?" At first you answer a patient, "No, not yet." You might even smile at the familiarity of the situation. But by the fourth, ninth, and sixteenth times, you're dangerously close to pulling the car over and making everyone else walk.

Been there? So has God. Consider the prayers He often hears. Can you fix this problem now, Lord? Where's the healing I've been asking for? I need an answer about the job today, God. Are You even listening? But His ways are not our ways—thankfully! Like you in the car, He knows that "we aren't there yet." Instead of frustrated threats to end the journey, He provides kindness and mercy when you approach His throne. Because of your high priest, Jesus, you can be assured that God hears your requests (Hebrews 4:14–15). When His answer is "no" or "not yet," He wants you to be confident that He will provide the kindness and mercy you need to be sustained. His boundless grace can move you from "Are we there yet?" to "Let's enjoy the ride together, Lord." Are you willing to trust His timing?

Like Rain and Snow

Rain and snow come down from the sky. They do not go back
again until they water the earth. They make it sprout and grow
so that it produces seed for farmers and food for people to eat. My
word, which comes from my mouth, is like the rain and snow.

Isaiah 55:10–11

When you awoke this morning, did you find yourself praying,
"Lord, I have this to do today and that and the other. Help me
accomplish all that I need to do and may my plans succeed."

It's not a bad prayer. Of course you want God to bless and
prosper the work you have before you each day.

Think about the words He spoke through the prophet Isaiah,
though. "'My thoughts are not your thoughts, and my ways are
not your ways,' declares the Lord. 'Just as the heavens are higher
than the earth, so my ways are higher than your ways, and my
thoughts are higher than your thoughts'" (Isaiah 55:8–9).

It's natural to want God to help and to answer your prayers
in the ways that you think best. After all, you're only human.

But, you see, that's the point. You're not God. His thoughts
are different than yours and His way of working in your world is
unique. You do not possess His omniscience or His omnipresence,
so how could you possibly know what is best in every situation?

Actually, the best prayer of all is the one in which you ask for
your will to come into alignment with His.

A Want or a Need?

My God will richly fill your every need in a glorious way through Christ Jesus.

Philippians 4:19

When you were a kid, perhaps a parent taught you the difference between a want and a need. God is also invested in your knowing the difference. He knows what you need and what you want. For example, you may want a zippy, cute little red convertible, but you really just need reliable transportation. You might want some expensive Italian slingbacks, but all you really need is a pair of moderately priced (but still attractive) shoes. You get the picture.

And then there are those below-the-surface needs that you may not even be aware that you have. You may need to be taken out of your comfort zone in order to grow. Maybe you need an abundant measure of forgiveness for a sin you didn't even realize you committed. And you might desperately need a divine touch of joy in a life that has become gray so gradually that you hardly noticed.

Through the divinely inspired words of the apostle Paul, you have the assurance that God knows your needs—even the ones you're not conscious of. And He's so faithful to fill those needs richly—beyond your wildest hopes. When you trust God completely to meet all your needs, He may even take care of a few wants—such as a 75 percent off sale on those slingbacks!

But even if you don't always get what you want, you will always have what you need. And that's infinitely better.

Making Negatives Positives

Finally, brothers and sisters, keep your thoughts on whatever is right or deserves praise: things that are true, honorable, fair, pure, acceptable, or commendable.

Philippians 4:8

Back in the day before digital, everyone used cameras that needed little canisters of film. You loaded the camera, advanced the film, pointed, focused, shot the pictures. After you got home, you took the film canister and, gingerly and hopefully, turned it over to the local drugstore. A few days later, you picked up the packet with (hopefully) terrific pictures of your family fun time. Tucked inside the envelope with the pictures were the negatives that were developed from the canister and then changed into "positives"—photos. The negatives could be used to order reprints of favorite pictures.

The apostle Paul describes another way of turning a negative into a positive: "Keep your thoughts on whatever is right." Focusing on the positive takes discipline. Instead of focusing on what you fear God is not doing, consider what you know to be true. For example, God

- is good no matter how bad the circumstances might be (Luke 18:19).
- promises never to leave or forsake you (Hebrews 13:5).
- urges you to "turn all your anxiety over to God because he cares for you" (1 Peter 5:7).

Consider also the "snapshots" of your life—the times when God proved Himself trustworthy. Why not load the camera of your mind's eye with these images as you offer God some praise?

The Answer to Fear

In the morning you'll say, "If only it were evening!" And in the evening you'll say, "If only it were morning!" You'll talk this way because of the things that will terrify you and because of the things you'll see.

Deuteronomy 28:67

With acts of violence peppering the news reports, it's easy to explain why people of the twenty-first century lead fearful lives. Watching the evening news in living color allows the evil in the world to parade through your living room. Why aren't the headlines announcing good news? Fear sells. It also steals away your sense of safety.

A lack of security combined with dissatisfaction with life is enough to make one echo the restless thoughts described in the above passage in Deuteronomy: "It's morning. If only it were evening!" Later, when darkness comes one says, "It's evening. If only it were morning!" What a terrible cycle to be in!

Do you find yourself in a cycle of fear? If so, you need the ultimate fear crusher—the Word of God. Many Bible verses assure you of God's protection in times of danger. For example: "Even when I am afraid, I still trust you. I praise the word of God. I trust God. I am not afraid" (Psalm 56:3–4).

As you are falling asleep this evening, concentrate on the loving, protective care of God your Father. Meditate on the words of a favorite hymn. Trust God to keep you safe. Bask in His presence. Release your worries to Him and go to sleep.

The Secret Ingredient

I'm not saying this because I'm in any need. . . . I've learned the secret of how to live when I'm full or when I'm hungry, when I have too much or when I have too little. I can do everything through Christ who strengthens me.

Philippians 4:11–13

Ever quiz a relative or a friend on a secret ingredient he or she adds to a dish or a sauce that makes it so special? "Come on! Was it allspice? Cardamom? Cinnamon?" More than likely, he or she refused to give up the secret. After all, it is a secret ingredient. But sometimes a relative might allow a few people in on the secret after some gentle arm-twisting. Perhaps you've been the recipient of one or two of these secret recipes that are now treasured pieces of your family's legacy.

The apostle Paul knew of a very different "secret ingredient"—one that is the hallmark of a life pleasing to God. Instead of keeping it secret, he wanted to share it with anyone who would listen. Paul's secret? We know it by one word: contentment. Paul knew that money, physical well-being, or relationships could not guarantee happiness. Having experienced tremendous hardships in life, among them beatings, shipwrecks, and false imprisonment, he relied on Christ's strength to navigate through these turbulent waters. Paul remained content, thanks to the belief that God was in his corner.

God is in your corner, too. Discover the same secret of contentment for yourself as you live according to God's Word. And that's a secret too good to keep to yourself.

Put Them in a Box

But I know that my defender lives, and afterwards, he will rise on the earth. Even after my skin has been stripped off my body, I will see God in my own flesh. I will see him with my own eyes, not with someone else's.

Job 19:25–27

Some evenings we feel abandoned and helpless in our search for answers to our problems.

You're not the first person to feel abandoned and alone. The words of today's Scripture reading were spoken by Job in the middle of his "bad day" story—the day four messengers told him the terrible news. Different groups of raiders carried off his oxen, donkeys, and camels, then killed his servants. A huge blaze consumed his sheep. Worst news of all: his seven sons and three daughters died after the room they were in collapsed. (See 1:13–22.)

Job sat humiliated and forlorn on an ash heap, his whole body afflicted with sores. He could find neither rest nor sleep. His friends accused him of sinning and his wife suggested that he "curse God and die!" (2:9). But Job handled his difficulties in a manner available to you today: he trusted God to be his defender. Through his suffering, he faithfully believed God would stand with him and give him the hope and strength he needed to survive his plight.

You can follow Job's example. Imagine you are standing in front of an empty box. In your mind place each of your problems in the box. Close the lid, and hand the box to God. Even though your fears might tell you otherwise, trust that God can handle anything inside that box.

Our Sun and Shield

The LORD God is a sun and shield. The LORD grants favor and honor. He does not hold back any blessing from those who live innocently.

Psalm 84:11

At times the sun's rays are so strong that our attempts to block them are useless. We've all been there. We're driving (seemingly) straight into the sun. We're wearing our sunglasses, struggling to position the car visor just right, but still the glare penetrates. We squint, shield our eyes, and try to navigate. Yet the sun prevails.

"The Lord God is a sun . . ." God prevails too. He penetrates. The light of His truth glares.

But, "The Lord God is . . . [also] a shield." He knows when to give us a reprieve. He protects us from the elements. He sends clouds to shade us. He orders cool breezes to refresh us. God understands the difficulty of contending with the sun. He knows when we need to stop and simply rest in His presence.

In a little while, your daily obligations will beckon you. Perhaps you have children to drive to school or you might be heading off to housework or the office. None of us know what the next twelve hours will bring. But God knows every conversation you will have and every circumstance you will encounter. He will determine if you need the light of His truth or the strength of His shield to protect you from the glare of false truth. So pack your sunglasses (just in case) and face the day with confidence. Because whether the sun is shining or the clouds are brewing, favor, honor, and blessing await you!

The Best Caregiver

When I look at your heavens, the creation of your fingers, the moon and the stars that you have set in place—what is a mortal that you remember him or the Son of Man that you take care of him?

Psalm 8:3–4

The Bible describes God's primary nature as all-powerful, all-knowing, present everywhere, and all-loving. No Bible translation, however, uses the word *caregiver* to describe God.

In today's society, a caregiver is defined as a person whose life is in some way restricted by the responsibility of caring for the needs of a child or dependent adult. In fact, with the aging of the world's population, the need for caregivers has created thriving businesses that provide professional caregivers. Magazines, support groups, newsletters, websites, and books are available to encourage and help parents, spouses, and family members with their care-giving duties.

Although He's never restricted, God is the ultimate Caregiver. David, the psalmist, knew this intimately, having been on the ragged edge of desperation for many years thanks to enemies and family problems. In this passage from Psalm 8, David asks why the Creator of the universe remembers and cares for each human being. The answer is simple: God loves us.

So what kind of care do you need tonight? Are you feeling worn out, stressed out, afraid, or alone? Before you fall asleep, reach out to God in prayer. He's waiting for you to ask for help right now, for He is the best Caregiver of all.

Quiet Whispering Voice

After the earthquake there was a fire. But the LORD wasn't in the fire. And after the fire there was a quiet, whispering voice. When Elijah heard it, he wrapped his face in his coat, went out, and stood at the entrance of the cave.

1 Kings 19:12–13

As Elijah fought to uphold God's covenant, he feared for his life, thanks to threats by Queen Jezebel and his urgent need for protection and direction. The voice of the Lord, in its quiet strength, calmed the powerful wrath of the raging storm within Elijah's spirit. God's voice became a beacon for the next step in His faithful servant's journey.

From the moment your feet hit the floor to begin each day anew, storms threaten your spiritual resilience. These storms, whether minor setbacks to the daily agenda or major life-threatening tragedies, can send you into a dizzying search for which way is up. Everyday obstacles upset the normal rhythms that sustain forward momentum, causing your faith to dwindle and leaving you to question your purpose. From sunrise to sunset, the sturdiness of your spiritual foundation is undoubtedly being challenged.

Are you sensing a storm brewing? Amidst the storm clouds of your day, allow God's quiet whispering voice to center your thoughts and actions for every step forward. Stop to find that place of stillness where the peace and grace of the Lord abounds. Know that in the eye of each storm you face today, God is speaking to soothe and strengthen your spirit.

Prayer of the Privileged

Morning, noon, and night I complain and groan, and he listens to my voice.

Psalm 55:17

You planned for a day as pleasant as a babbling brook. You got a torrential river experience instead. Bad traffic made you late for your first appointment. Another client was a no-show. The kids wouldn't stop arguing. Later on, a good friend called to tell you bad news. Your day definitely merits complaints and groans.

But there is good news. You have a standing invitation to communicate with God. Grab hold of the privilege of prayer. You can pray in any position: standing up, lying down, sitting, kneeling, or even flopped down and sprawled out on the sofa—eyes open or eyes closed. He listens to your voice, whether you whisper in a barely audible voice or just groan in sorrow.

Begin your prayer tonight with a thankful heart toward an amazing God who has the power to handle your life's glitches. Lay your biggest need before Him—the one for which you have no solution. Believe in the impossible—that God can bring something good out of a terrible circumstance.

Now slip into bed, confident that God has heard your voice because you answered His invitation to the privilege of conversation with Him in prayer.

Welcome

The LORD is my light and my salvation. Who is there to fear?
The LORD is my life's fortress. Who is there to be afraid of?

Psalm 27:1

Do not be afraid! Do not worry!

When you were a child, your mom or your dad could fix any problem, kiss any bruise, soothe any fear. Any anxiety you felt disappeared in the light of day and, with a hug from Mom, you went on your merry way. Life was simple.

What happened? Your fears and worries kept pace with your growing responsibilities. Perhaps today, decisions weigh heavily upon you and you long to have some measure of control over the unknown.

Consider King David's abundant confidence in the Lord throughout Psalm 27. If anyone had reason to feel uncertain about life's twists and turns, David did. Remember the trials David faced: his best friend's father tried to kill him, and later his own son, Absalom, rose against him. In spite of all this, David trusted in God's love, mercy, and forgiveness. He boldly proclaims, "The Lord is my light and my salvation. Who is there to fear?" He knew that the light of God's love would guide and protect him.

There is no uncertainty for your Father. He knows what every moment will bring. Do not let the fear of the unknown rule you. Instead, let your heavenly Father banish that fear this morning, just as your own mother or father would have done. Let Him be your place of refuge, allowing you to boldly ask, "Who is there to fear?" You are welcome there.

Song in the Night

I remember my song in the night and reflect on it. . . . I will remember the deeds of the Lord. I will remember your ancient miracles. I will reflect on all your actions and think about what you have done.

Psalm 77:6, 11–12

Nighttime. A time of precious rest. All too often, however, it can be a time of distress. You lay your head on the pillow only to be assaulted by fear and pain that decides to engage you just as you seek to find quiet. Your mind has been whirling all day, busy with the activities of your life, without room to consider fearful thoughts. But when it's finally dark and quiet . . .

That's when you need a song in the night. That's when you need—to paraphrase the psalm—to reflect on all of God's actions and think about what He has done.

Asaph, writer of this psalm, knew about songs. He was, after all, an important tabernacle musician as well as the author of several psalms. Songs were his passion, his life's work, his calling. Beyond these duties, Asaph also wrote of having a song in the night. Perhaps he was onto something.

What's whirling in your mind tonight? What threatens to keep you tossing and turning? Take a few moments now to petition Jesus to give you a song in the night. Maybe it's a literal praise song you can sing to yourself that will focus your mind on the deeds of the Lord. Maybe it's a passage of Scripture memorized long ago and deeply ingrained in the recesses of your mind.

Then let your song in the night sing you to sleep.

Confident Hope

I will always have hope. I will praise you more and more.

Psalm 71:14

Hope is waiting expectantly at the airport as passengers disembark. Hope is the gentle touch of a hand in a moment of pain. Hope is the promise of new life in baby's first cry. Hope is sunlight at dawn, smell of fresh rain, spring's first bud. Hope is the gift that gives life to all who receive it.

We are blessed because we can cling to the hope that God has given to us through His Son, Jesus Christ. When it feels so very dark, when it appears that there is no way out, if we pause for just one moment and look, really look, we can see a place where hope resides. Even if it seems very small or very far away, there is a hope beyond our understanding—a hope that is placed there just for us.

Reach out your hand, extend your heart and receive the hope that has been offered to you. Grab hold, cling tight. Draw near to Him, and He will draw near to you. He will uphold you. He will guide you. He will protect you. And He will continue loving you. You are not alone.

You can have complete confidence in the hope He gives. As the apostle Peter wrote, "We have been born into a new life that has a confidence which is alive because Jesus Christ has come back to life. We have been born into a new life which has an inheritance that can't be destroyed or corrupted and can't fade away. That inheritance is kept in heaven for you" (1 Peter 1:3–4).

Living God's Way

At midnight I wake up to give thanks to you for the regulations, which are based on your righteousness.

Psalm 119:62

You probably learned at an early age that rules govern your life. In preschool, you needed to put your belongings in your cubbyhole. Grade school introduced a whole new set of rules such as "Put your homework in the red basket." In high school you were issued your driver's license after you passed a test on driving regulations. As an adult, other regulations rule your life: Pay your power bill on time or the electricity gets cut off; pay your taxes on time or you will have to pay a fine; get your kids vaccinated before they start school.

Your walk with God also includes regulations. The writer of Psalm 119 uses many different words for regulations. The most frequently used word is *torah*, which can mean "teaching" or "instruction" or "law." Other words are *principles*, *commandments*, *word*, and *promise*. Simply put, God gave you directions that describe how to live a life that is pleasing to Him. In Psalm 119, the psalmist thanks God for His regulations.

Do you approach God's rules with the same thankfulness? God always appreciates it when you thank Him for His guidance in your life. Before you sleep this evening, why not tell God how grateful you are for His clear, biblical instructions. Sleep in peace, for God loves a grateful heart.

Morning Announcements

It is good to announce your mercy in the morning and your faithfulness in the evening.

Psalm 92:2

What does your alarm clock announce to you first thing in the morning? Probably not "mercy" (as the verse suggests). It's more like, "Get up! Hurry up! You'll be late! Stop hitting the snooze button!" Announcements with exclamation points all the way.

If your alarm could announce mercy, you might think it would decide to go off when it sensed you starting to awaken. Then it would softly cajole you with your favorite quiet tunes. Nice, huh? But you would rarely get out of bed on time. Alarm clocks gotta do what they gotta do. We need them for just that purpose.

Once out of bed, however, you can open God's Word and listen to His announcements of mercy to you as the writer of Psalm 92 suggests. Another announcement of mercy comes from the stylus of the apostle Paul who wrote, "God is rich in mercy because of his great love for us. We were dead because of our failures, but he made us alive together with Christ" (Ephesians 2:4–5). Now that's an announcement worth getting out of bed for!

This morning, consider God's announcement of mercy toward you. Then ask Him to show you how to announce His mercy to those you meet today.

A Cry for Help

The LORD is near to everyone who prays to him, to every faithful person who prays to him. He fills the needs of those who fear him. He hears their cries for help and saves them.

Psalm 145:18–19

Nothing tugs at the heart quite like the sound of a crying child. Your brain kicks into action with a set of questions: Is the child hungry? Tired? Hurt? Afraid? If it's your child, you go as quickly as you can to check out his/her needs. If it's not your child, you look around for the child's caregiver. You become concerned if the crying doesn't cease, if you sense the child's needs aren't being met. You can't really relax until the sound stops.

When you decided to follow Jesus, you became a child of God. Does that mean you will never again experience troubles or sorrow or pain? No. It means you have full access to God, the true source of life. God hears every cry uttered by His children loud and clear. This is David's message in Psalm 145. It was one David fully believed in. The book of Psalms is filled with David's cries for help.

Before you sleep tonight, praise God for three situations in which you felt His intervention and power. Praise Him for His presence. Freely share your current needs with Him. For just as a mother seeks to still her child's cry, God stands ready to give you the peace and rest your heart desires.

Dawn's Early Light

I got up before dawn, and I cried out for help. My hope is based on your word.

Psalm 119:147

Have you ever experienced a sleepless night? Maybe you were able to finally fall asleep after tossing and turning for a few hours, only to wake up two hours before the alarm and not be able to fall back to sleep again. So after pounding your pillow, you got up in the darkness and awaited the dawn—knowing that the coming day was going to be very long indeed.

The psalmist was troubled because lawless people were coming to attack him; yet he took courage in knowing that God always keeps His promises. He prayed to the Lord and turned the situation over to Him.

In those early morning hours, you too can cry out to God for help, knowing that your hope is based on His Word. God doesn't want you to be in a constant state of worry. He doesn't want you to be awakening before you've had enough rest simply because the worries are keeping your mind from sleep.

Yet, because God is a gentleman, He is not going to barge in and take over your life without being invited. When you worry, you assume you can control the circumstances and situation. But when you pray and ask for God's intervention, you remind yourself that He is in complete control. And you invite Him not only to work out everything according to His will, but you allow His peace to comfort you and bring the hope you need—for today and every day.

To Plan or Not to Plan?

Do not brag about tomorrow, because you do not know what another day may bring.

Proverbs 27:1

Ever make plans that were thwarted by an outcome you didn't predict? We all have times when we think we know what tomorrow might bring. This verse in Proverbs is played out in a parable Jesus tells in the Gospel of Luke. In that story, a rich man made plans to build larger barns in which to store his abundant crops. His plans for the future, however, were in vain, as God announced that the man would die that night.

Does this mean that making plans for your future is wrong? No. Go ahead and prepare a budget, work schedule, or a move to another place. But be sure to allow for God's guidance as you plan. Jeremiah 29:11 explains why this is so important: "I know the plans that I have for you, declares the LORD. They are plans for peace and not disaster, plans to give you a future filled with hope."

As you get ready for bed tonight, do you have doubts about your future plans? It's not the time to be self-reliant. Pray for wisdom and direction from God regarding the course your life should take. He may guide you down an unexpected path—a path you might never have anticipated or chosen on your own. And because you don't know what tomorrow may bring, how wonderful to go to sleep tonight entrusting tomorrow to the One who does know.

Future Vision

Entrust your efforts to the LORD, and your plans will succeed.
Proverbs 16:3

Every day you make plans or put forth effort toward something—be it a job, schooling, raising children, doing volunteer work. Effort plus plan equals success (at least that's what we want to believe).

Proverbs indicates that the above equation is true, with one caveat: We are to entrust our efforts to the Lord, and then our plans will succeed.

What's going on in your life—not today, but long range? Beyond today's schedule and activities, what does life look like "out there" in the somewhat distant future? Where do you want to be in a year? five years? ten years? What visions are springing to life in your heart?

Everyone wonders what the future holds. Some seek out blindly to discover the future by trusting in horoscopes and Tarot card readings. How wonderful that you don't need to resort to those dead-end attempts at knowing the future. Instead, you can be in contact this morning with the One who knows exactly where you'll be next year, in five years, in ten years. He's not going to lay it out for you, but He is going to guide you on the steps today that will take you in the direction He wants you to go.

So the dreams you have for the future? Lay them before God today.

Such Treasures to Behold!

Therefore, a time of rest and worship exists for God's people.
Hebrews 4:9

Have you ever had a time when one crisis after another seemed to occur? Everyone has such times periodically. Maybe that's why God made the commandment to set a whole day aside for rest, as this verse in Hebrews mentions.

If it's true we all have trials, it is also true that we all have treasures! Slowing down helps us see the great riches we have received. No matter what problems you are dealing with now, when you reflect on all God's gifts, you'll feel refreshed and renewed.

Our gifts from God are magnificent. The gift of our amazingly complex bodies can inspire us. The gift of family can comfort us. The gift of creation, in all its regal forms, calls out for attention. The gifts of a warm house, inspiring words to read, a soft quilt, an aromatic cup of tea—these are blessings we can feel, smell, and appreciate.

Imagine how a treasure hunter rejoices over the discovery of jewels. Just think—your God-given treasure box is always available. At this time of night, you can remember the commandment to rest. With your treasure box of blessings from God open to appreciate, you can relax easily. Settle into bed like a queen. What a wonder it is to have been lavished with so many blessings.

Open your treasure box now. Dig deeply into this bounty of heavenly gifts.

The Sun's Rays

His brightness is like the sunlight. Rays of light stream from his hand. That is where his power is hidden.

Habakkuk 3:4

Have you ever felt as if your questions fall on deaf ears? Maybe you wonder why the bad things happening in the world are allowed to happen at all or why so many diseases can't be cured.

The prophet Habakkuk had those same questions. He saw the world around him crumbling under the weight of sin and it broke his heart. In the first chapter of the book named for him, he urgently plies God with question upon question. In the beginning of the second chapter, however, he waits patiently for God's answer. And God doesn't leave him hanging. His answer comes like a ray of sunshine, rolling back the dark cloud of confusion.

As God explains, the wicked will be judged and justice will prevail. Peace might not come as quickly as the prophet desires, but it will come all the same. This short book concludes with a prayer of praise. Habakkuk recognizes the awesome power of God and thanks Him for His promise of strength for the dark days ahead.

This small, obscure book of the Old Testament gives the perfect example of how to conduct your prayer life. Whatever concerns are on your heart, ask God about them. He will hear the questions. Then, quietly wait. God's answer will come. When it does, whether it's what you were hoping or not, praise Him for His faithfulness to you. Thank Him for listening and being willing to work in your life.

A Brilliant Message

Look at the sky and see. Who created these things? Who brings out the stars one by one? He calls them all by name.

Isaiah 40:26

It's the work of an artist—carefully crafted, piece by piece, down to every detail. What was He thinking, this artist-God, as He painted the sky with these billions of clusters of gaseous light? Imagine Him smiling as He looked at all that He had created. Knowing the life span of each ball of fire, He also knew the wonder and amazement that we, His children, would feel as we look up. It's too big for us to imagine, but not for Him. Even the millions and billions of stars are not overwhelming to our Father. He knows them by name. He knows their size, their exact location, their history, and not only that: He created them all. And He created you.

Whenever you doubt if God knows what frustrations you face, look at the sky and see. Look up. If you're unsure if God truly has your best interests in mind, look up. When life gets overwhelming and it feels like you're all alone, stop, and look up.

Every night, your Father is sending you a brilliant message of His love for you. He's shouting His greatness and care for you. In the evening, even in the darkness of night, you are not alone. You have a Father who loves you and is powerful enough to provide for you. He knows your name and wishes you a good night's rest.

By the Stream

Blessed is the person who trusts the LORD. . . . He will be like a tree that is planted by water. It will send its roots down to a stream. It will not be afraid in the heat of summer. Its leaves will turn green. It will not be anxious during droughts. It will not stop producing fruit.

Jeremiah 17:7–8

The source for a healthy tree is in its roots. Healthy roots mean a healthy tree.

Roots are meant to go deep and spread out wide into the soil. Roots are the pathway through which the life-giving water and nutrients reach the tree. If a tree's roots are not healthy then it cannot receive the nourishment it needs to thrive and survive. The tree weakens and may eventually die in times of drought or storms.

Likewise, our spiritual health cannot thrive or even survive without healthy spiritual roots founded in spiritual disciplines. By practicing such disciplines as reading Scripture, prayer, silence and solitude, acts of service, and fasting, we can cultivate our spiritual roots and encourage them to grow deep so that God can nourish us with His living waters. And as He nourishes us, we grow stronger in our spirit. This strength allows us to maintain a healthy faith in times of spiritual drought or in dire circumstances. At times when we would most likely weaken and fall, we can remain strong and even continue to produce spiritual fruit through the strength and nourishment that God has given to us through healthy spiritual roots.

How well cultivated are your spiritual roots? Are you drawing water from the stream of God's Word? The tree planted by the water will survive anything. So can you.

Peace beyond Understanding

I'm leaving you peace. I'm giving you my peace. I don't give you the kind of peace that the world gives. So don't be troubled or cowardly.

John 14:27

All around us, we're bombarded with cries for peace or peaceful solutions to problems. We see peace symbols on jewelry or scrawled across signs, but peace never really comes.

That's why Jesus promised His peace, which is not of this world. Although He would soon be killed, His death would bring about the ultimate peace—a reconciliation between God and man. The prophet Isaiah saw it centuries before: "He was wounded for our rebellious acts. He was crushed for our sins. He was punished so that we could have peace, and we received healing from his wounds" (Isaiah 53:5).

Jesus' peace does not mean absence of conflict. His peace does not mean quiet solace for the rest of our lives. It's a different kind of peace, not the peace the world might attempt to give, or peace as the world would define it. Instead, it's a deep inner core of peace in the midst of conflict, in the center of difficulty, in the eye of the storm. This peace grounds you, holds you, protects you, helps you keep it together on the inside no matter what's going on outside.

Are you in need of peace? Meditate on Jesus' promise of peace. He said to His disciples, and to you, "I've told you this so that my peace will be with you. In the world you'll have trouble. But cheer up! I have overcome the world" (John 16:33).

Whatever I Want?

This is what will be done for someone who doesn't doubt but believes what he says will happen: He can say to this mountain, "Be uprooted and thrown into the sea," and it will be done for him. That's why I tell you to have faith that you have already received whatever you pray for, and it will be yours.

Mark 11:22–24

As a child you probably read stories of genies or fairies who promised to grant the wishes of a blessed few because they rubbed magic lamps or were simply in the right place at the right time. Their lives were forever changed by the encounter with this powerful being. Perhaps you envied the fact that they had carte blanche—full authority—to ask for whatever they wanted.

Peter's life was forever changed by an encounter with the most powerful being of all—God. He too was told that he had full authority to ask for whatever he desired. Imagine how startling and perplexing Jesus' announcement might have sounded. The wheels begin to turn in the human brain as we think about how to turn this invitation to our advantage. But note the bottom line that Jesus mentions: "Have faith in God." Faith is the key that moves mountains—faith and the knowledge of God's desires. You see, everything hinges on God. Although He has the power to do the impossible (for example, removing a mountain), everything He does fits neatly within His will. He just wants His people to take courage and ask.

What are the mountains in your life that need removing? A mountain can be any obstacle that stands between you and a goal you have. Are you willing to ask for its removal and also to trust that God will act in a way that's best for you?

Resolved to Wait

I will look to the LORD. I will wait for God to save me. I will wait for my God to listen to me.

Micah 7:7

Waiting is hard. As children, we all struggled with waiting. We wanted Christmas to come tomorrow, wanted dessert before dinner, and wanted our turn on the swing to be right now, rather than once our brother or sister was done.

Now, even though we're "all grown up," waiting isn't easier. Sometimes we're waiting for things that are urgent—the tax refund or that next paycheck to arrive, a phone call about that new job or commission, or a loved one to come home safely. When Micah speaks of waiting in these verses, he's not talking about waiting for ice cream or a turn on the monkey bars. He, too, is waiting for something truly important. He's waiting for his people to be freed from oppression, to be given their lives and country back.

Is it easy to wait? Absolutely not, but Micah resolves in his heart that he "will wait" because he knows that the only real answer to his worries comes from above. This is an example of waiting with anticipation. He knows that something good is about to happen. It's like the waiting for the fireworks to start on the Fourth of July. You have no doubt that you'll see them across the sky.

What are you waiting for? Will you trust God to answer in His time? Can you say with confidence that His timing is perfect, even when it seems otherwise from your perspective? Pray that He will give you that confidence tonight.

Hang On Tight

*Those who suffer because that is God's will for them must entrust
themselves to a faithful creator and continue to do what is good.*

1 Peter 4:19

What have you been asking God for? How long have you prayed?
Are you beginning to wonder when—or if—your prayer will be
answered?

Is discouragement or suffering making you wonder, Are my
requests hitting a brick wall? Is God apathetic? Is He slow? Is He
playing a cruel game of waiting to see how long I can hold on?
Be honest; we all have seasons of doubt. God isn't threatened
by your qualms. He made you and understands human limitations. Through the ages, the Bible reveals faithful believers who
agonized or fumed or waited . . . on God.

It's difficult to always keep a praise attitude, especially when
it seems you're just trying to hang on. There's no indication He's
helping. You hear platitudes like, "God is working on the other
end," or "Have faith. God's timing is always perfect." Deep down,
you know that's true, but it still demands sheer grit to trust and
to obey and to "continue to do what is good." You may feel like
the cat stuck up in the tree, waiting for rescue. You just grip onto
the truth that God is faithful—and you hang on for dear life.

And you know what? That's okay. Hold on, friend. Entrust
yourself and your needs to your heavenly Father. Preoccupy yourself with doing good. Soon you'll be hoisted back onto solid
ground.

Deposits in God's Bank

My eyes are wide-open throughout the nighttime hours to reflect on your word.

Psalm 119:148

For some, a sleepless night is the ultimate enemy to wrestle against and hopefully win. But for the writer of Psalm 119, a sleepless night was filled with the potential for connecting with God. In Psalm 119:145–146, he pleaded with the Lord to save him. "I have called out with all my heart. Answer me, O LORD. I want to obey your laws. I have called out. Save me, so that I can obey your written instructions." A few verses later, he explained how he spent the time reflecting on God's Word. Believing that the Lord would guide him, he praised the Lord for His goodness and vowed to obey His laws.

Note that he didn't spend the time grumbling about wakefulness. After all, wakefulness seemed to be a conscious choice in order to commune with God. Instead, he took his worry and deposited it in his heavenly Father's bank, then "withdrew" the truths of God's Word.

What keeps you awake at night? Worries? Pain? Anticipation for what tomorrow might bring? Tonight, ask God to help you dwell on His promises. He promises to love you, guide you, and answer you. Why not make a withdrawal from God's bank of wisdom and promises? Enter that place of wonder. Discover the exhilaration of following Christ!

Contributors

Judith Costello
Heather Cox
Jennifer Devlin
Carol Chaffee Fielding
Kathy Hardee
Jennifer A. Haynes
Elizabeth C. Hubbard
Pat Stockett Johnston
Kathy Lay
Frances L. Lewis
Diane Markins
Brenda Nixon
Erin P. O'Connor
Heather M. Pleier
Robin Priestley
Sue Rosenfeld
Marggie Wallem Rowe
Hilary S. Sahli
Debbie Simler-Goff
Alene Snodgrass
Kathryn A. Spurgeon
Amber E. Susek
Ann Swindell
Michelle Van Loon
Linda Washington

Encouragement to
Start and End the Day

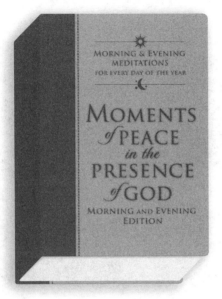

This 365-day devotional features two readings for every day—
one for morning and one for evening. With imitation leather
binding and a ribbon marker, this treasury of meditations is
perfect for any gift-giving occasion.

Praise Him in the morning with these 170 moving reflections, devotional thoughts, and encouraging Scriptures. And don't let the sun go down without celebrating the gifts God gives us with these 170 inspirational thoughts and prayers to end your day.

MEDITATIONS ON
WISDOM FROM THE BIBLE

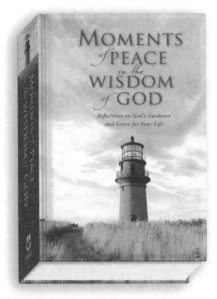

Find a respite from the pace and stress of life
with these inspiring selections from the Proverbs
and other wisdom passages.

A BEAUTIFUL DEVOTIONAL
FOR COUPLES

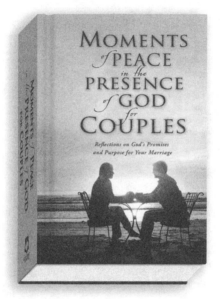

This 365-day devotional features two readings for every day—one for morning and one for evening—and offers biblical wisdom that couples can easily apply to the challenges of today.

a division of Baker Publishing Group
www.BethanyHouse.com

Available wherever books are sold.

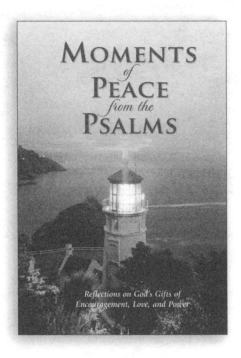

MOMENTS
of
PEACE
from the
PSALMS

*Reflections on God's Gifts of
Encouragement, Love, and Power*

This soul-replenishing and spiritually renewing
collection of reflections and prayers from the
Psalms will motivate you every day to use the
gifts God gave you.